Tell All the Children Our Story

Tell All the Children Our Story

Memories and Mementos of Being Young and Black in America

Tonya Bolden

Harry N. Abrams, Inc., Publishers, New York

Editor: Howard W. Reeves
Designer: Edward Miller

You may visit Tonya Bolden's website at www.tonyabolden.com

Library of Congress Cataloging-in-Publication Data

Bolden, Tonya.
    Tell all the children our story : memories and mementos of being young
and Black in America / by Tonya Bolden.
        p. cm.
    ISBN 0-8109-4496-0
    1. African American children—History—Juvenile literature. 2. African American children—Social conditions—Juvenile
literature. 3. African American children—Biography—Juvenile literature. 4. United States—Race relations—Juvenile literature.
[1. African Americans. 2. African Americans—History. 3. Race relations.] I. Title.
E185.86 .B633 2002
973'.0496073—dc21

                                    2001001353

Harry N. Abrams, Inc.
100 Fifth Avenue
New York, N.Y. 10011
www.abramsbooks.com

One of the many Adinkra symbols, associated with the Akan of Ghana and the Gyaman of Côte d'Ivoire. This one is a version of the symbol for *sankofa*, which literally means "return and pick it up," and on a deeper level, "one must return to the past to move forward."

Page 1: An unidentified South Carolinian, photographed by Richard Samuel Roberts in the 1920s. Page 2: Langston Hughes (c. 1919) with his friends Isidor Kaplow, Wendel Gomez, and Irwin Braverman. All four boys attended Central High School in Cleveland, Ohio, where Hughes toyed with becoming a graphic artist, ran track, and contributed poems and short stories to the school magazine he edited, *The Monthly*.

Contents

Acknowledgments 6

Preface 9

Part I: Out of Africa 11

Part II: Longing for the Jubilee 29

Part III: Lift Every Voice and Sing 63

Notes 118

Selected Bibliography 122

Suggested Reading 123

Illustration Credits 123

Index 126

Acknowledgments

I am profoundly grateful to—and for—my editor on this book, Howard Reeves, for his unflagging faith in this project, for his acuity and curiosity, for his super sensibilities and skills. Many thanks, too, to other members of the Abrams family: Laaren Brown, Amy Corley, John Crowley, Amy Kaufman, Patti Nolan, Michele Riley, Becky Terhune, and certainly not least of all Emily Farbman, for helping me keep track of so many details. I am grateful to Ed Miller for his marvelous designing mind.

Thanks is also due to many old and new friends and acquaintances, some of whom read passages of the manuscript, some of whom helped with points of research, some of whom did both. They are: Donald Bogle, Herb Boyd, William Jelani Cobb, Elza Dinwiddie-Boyd, Marie Dutton Brown, Connie Green, David Hackley, Dianne Johnson, Ronda Racha Penrice, Suzanne Randolph, Judy Dothard Simmons, Bobby Thomas, and Velma Maia Thomas. As always, I am very appreciative for the assists of many people at my New York treasure, The Schomburg Center for Research in Black Culture, most especially Sharon Howard, James E. Huffman Jr., Diana Lachatanere, Tammi Lawson, Anthony Toussaint, and Mary Yearwood.

This book was also blessed with kindnesses of many strangers—people who took that extra step in response to an inquiry. Thank you, Jennifer Bean Bower (MESDA); Margaret Cook (Swem Library at William and Mary College); Cathy Ingram (Frederick Douglass National Historic Site); James E. Kennedy (University of South Alabama); Kathryn Meehan (South Carolina Historical Society); Alfred Mueller (Beineke Rare Book and Manuscript Library, Yale University), Betsy Rosasco (The Art Museum, Princeton University); Philip D. Morgan (Johns Hopkins University); Larry Mensching (Joslyn Art Museum); Ron Michener (University of Virginia); Jim Nance (University of Tennessee at Martin); Sally Stassi (Williams Research Center); Doug Tucker; John White (Southern Historical Collection, University of North Carolina); Sherri Wilkins (Stagville Historic Center); and at the Colonial Williamsburg Foundation, Catherine Grosfils, Martha Katz-Hyman, and William Pittman.

And then there's my base: Huge gratitude—kisses and hugs in plenitude—to Daddy, MaLou, Nelta, and Bobby. Thank you for all the on-going, ever-growing love and support.

My ultimate gratitude: to God, my provider and sustainer.

For all the children who have brought me joy
(some of whom are by now all grown up!) —especially . . .

Monica Aldana

Aamil Khali Brice

Nailah J. Bristow

Jennifer Brown

Bobby Brunson Jr.

Shawn Carter

Maileen Chaparro

Jose Duverge

Jordan William Freeland

Sydney and Courtney George

Dylan Hackley

Savannah-Re Haylette

Aisha Jefferson

Elizabeth Jenkins-Sahlin

Divivian Jerome-McGuire

Elizabeth Johnson

Amira and Jamil Karriem

Nadine, Eliza, and Marina Lehner

Catherine Llanos

Justin, Gabrielle, and Randy Logan

Kadisha McGuire

André Miller

Tamara Morgan

Cassandra Reyes

Abner Rodriguez

Joseph Roman

Gretchen Rosenkranz

Rafael Salas

Irene Santos

Marcus and Alexandro Shepard

Justin Smith

Porsha and Mia Solomon

Ja-Tun Thomas

Our Gang (1886) by Joseph Decker. This painting's original title was *Accused*. Its renaming in the 1930s may have been prompted by the popularity of the *Our Gang* movie shorts.

Preface

Having produced a few books touching on the history of black men and women in America, it seemed only natural that I turn my attention to boys and girls of African descent who have worked, played, been schooled, suffered, endured, and dreamed in America. Thus, this scrapbook, this witness of the black experience in miniature, if you will. This book does not claim to be comprehensive. Rather it is one writer's contribution to the telling of a rich and textured, very large, very long story.

Part I ("Out of Africa") takes up colonial America through the Revolutionary War; Part II ("Longing for the Jubilee"), the nineteenth century; and Part III ("Lift Every Voice and Sing"), the twentieth century. Each part opens with a bit of background on the period. The narrative within each part provides context for the mementos and remembrances, which include paintings, photographs, documents, ephemera, and patches of childhood memories from essays, interviews, and autobiographies.

Years ago I came across Margaret Burroughs's ardent poem, "What Shall I Tell My Children Who Are Black?" and ever since it has remained dear to my heart. *Tell All the Children Our Story* is in some way a call-and-response to this poem: a tribute, a celebration, a something that will, as Burroughs put it, make black youth "confident in the knowledge of [their] worth." As we all know, knowledge of one's history—the sorrow songs and the jubilees—is essential for self-worth, and for perspective.

As you can see from its title, this book is not for the black child only. For teachers, librarians, parents (or me) to suggest that it is so exclusive would be an insult to the intellects and curiosity of a rainbow of children. What's more, I never envisioned this book for the young only. My ideal reader is a family (in the broadest sense): two or more generations engaging with this book together, with adults sharing the memories and mementos of their own childhoods with the young and the young putting themselves in the shoes of boys and girls they meet in this book. May they be inspired to tell their own stories with a combination of words and images.

—*Tonya Bolden*

9

Two Boys in the Slave Fort from Tom Feelings's *Middle Passage: White Ships/Black Cargo* (1995). Prior to shipment across the Atlantic Ocean, countless Africans suffered confinement in a fort or "slave house" on the coast of West Africa, such as the one still standing on Senegal's Gorée Island.

PART I

Out of Africa

Only the ocean knows how many children and adults perished during the Middle Passage: that horrendous thirty- to ninety-day journey to the Americas. And there's no accounting of how many died before they left Africa—as they wept, bled, and grieved in long whip-, cudgel-, and gun-managed marches to the coast where slave ships waited. So it is that some say ten million, some say twenty million, some say upwards of sixty million African children, women, and men were snatched up for slavery.

This African holocaust began in the mid-1400s with the Portuguese and the Spanish, the lords of the trade, selling their captives to wealthy Europeans. In the early 1500s they began shipping Africans across the Atlantic Ocean to work gold mines, sugar plantations, and other enterprises in South America and the West Indies. "They" soon included the French, the Dutch, and the British.

The transport of Africans directly to Great Britain's North American mainland colonies became intense after 1672, the year King Charles II formed the Royal African Company. By the end of the seventeenth century Great Britain was king of the European slave trade.

As precious metals, timber, tobacco, rice, and other bounties of the Americas—reaped through slave labor—grew in demand in Europe, Africa was steadily drained of farmers, builders, merchants, artisans, priests, warriors, mothers, fathers, and children.

On January 3, 1624, roughly one hundred and fifty years before the birth of the United States, the child regarded as the first African American was baptized in Virginia: William Tucker.

William's parents, Isabell and Antoney, were among the Africans aboard a Dutch man-of-war that docked at marshy, mosquito-ridden Jamestown in late August 1619. They were among the "20. and odd Negroes" the ship's captain swapped for provisions.

Isabell and Antoney, whose African names are unknown, may have been born in what is today Angola, Ghana, Guinea, Nigeria, Senegal, Sierra Leone, or any number of other sub-Saharan African nations (whence the majority of kidnapped Africans came). The couple may have been Akan, Bakongo, Igbo, Mende, Wolof, Xhosa, or Yoruba. Had they known and wed each other in their homeland, they would have chosen, no doubt, an African name for their son, a name that commemorated something about his birth or hopes for his future—*Sekou* (warrior), *Obadele* (the king arrives), *Kodjo* (humorous), *Fanta* (born on a beautiful day), *Diallo* (he is bold), or perhaps *Baako* (first born). Instead, the baby was named William. This happened in Jamestown, when he was baptized into the Church of England, which at the time prohibited the enslavement of Christians.

Like other first Africans to dwell in mainland North America (and like many pauper Europeans), William's parents were not slaves but indentured servants. They were not owned but rather had to work, without wages, for a specific number of years for a particular person. Isabell and Antoney worked for Captain William Tucker of Elizabeth City, Virginia. At the end of their indenture, the couple was free to start a life of their own. They may have been aided in their new life with "freedom dues": homespun clothes or cloth, corn, and a little cash.

William's father did eventually own land, which young William would have helped clear and tend. What exactly William grew up to do for a living is unknown, but he did have children. So this first African born in mainland North

Opposite page: *Jamestown Landing* (1901) by Howard Pyle remembers the unloading, in late August 1619, of Africans from a Dutch warship at Jamestown, Virginia, the first permanent British settlement in mainland North America. These Africans had been pirated from a Spanish frigate en route to the West Indies, and among them were the parents of the first African born in what is now the United States.

Portrait of a Negro Girl and *Portrait of a Negro Boy* by Charles (some sources, Carolus) Zechel. Based on the subjects' attire, these oil-on-glass miniatures may be of youths living in mid-seventeenth-century New York (New Netherland at the time, and under Dutch control).

America was a witness, along with his offspring, of the beginning of the embrace of black slave labor by many of the English, Germans, Scots, Irish, Dutch, and other people intent on prospering, by any means necessary, in what would one day be the United States. Keeping black slaves was cheaper in the long run than having indentured servants and less troublesome than enslaving the Powhatan, Tuscarora, Yamasee, and other native peoples who, for one, knew the land and could, therefore, more easily escape.

Thus, colony after colony—Massachusetts in 1641, William's Virginia in 1661—legalized and encouraged the enslavement of blacks for the duration of their lives, or *durante vita*, as some documents put it.

Georgia was the last of Great Britain's North American colonies to say yes to slavery, in 1750. By then Virginia alone was importing upwards of one thousand

Africans annually, and it was no longer forbidden to enslave black Christians. What's more, given the increase in white men siring children with black women, to curb black freedom by birthright, the status of a black child no longer flowed from the father (as with a white child), but from the mother.

A Female Negro Child (of an extraordinary good Breed) to be given away, Inquire of Edes and Gill.

Boston Gazette. Feb 25. 1765.

This advertisement supports one colonial's observation that at one point in New England African children were given away "like puppies."

By the mid-eighteenth century the territory that became the thirteen colonies—a crazy quilt of laws, customs, and cultures—had a population of a little more than one million, with about 240,000 of the people in bondage. Only a small percent of the enslaved were children under the age of ten, and the conditions under which they lived varied.

A child purchased into a family with few or no other slaves might not fare too badly—might even be treated like family. However, one *born* into such a household might be an unplanned expense for the owner, one too many mouths to feed. Such unwanted babies were often sold, sometimes for a song, or as a colonial would say, for a "pistareen." Some children did not even cost that.

Owners of large plantations and other businesses generally needed ready labor: The purchase of adult slaves (mostly men) was their first priority. When they did buy a child, often he or she was a gift to a white child. Such was on the mind of Robert Carter—a Virginian who at one point owned more than seven hundred people—when in 1728 he laid plans to buy three girls: one for each of his young grandsons. "It would be like wealthy youngsters today getting an extravagant gift—a BMW car, for instance," explains historian Philip D. Morgan. "An insignia of affluence, gentlemanly status."

Training a child for life as a gentleman's valet or ladies' maid was sometimes the purpose of such a purchase. This was, presumably, the case with the ten-year-old boy and twelve-year-old girl who were the personal servants of George Washington's stepchildren, Jacky and Patsy, when they were in their teens. By giving black children to white children, adults were not only conditioning the black children for service, but also readying the white children to rule.

Top, left: *Henry Darnall III as a Child* (c. 1710) by Justus Engelhardt Kühn captures the gentry's ideal of the natural order between themselves and Africans. Most slaves, however, were dressed in castoffs or rags. Top, right: *Elias Ball II* (c. 1770) by Jeremiah Theus. Elias Ball II inherited a large estate from his father, who had arrived in Charles Town (later Charleston), South Carolina, in 1698 to take possession of property and people left him by an uncle.

Some wealthy slaveholders made a point of buying children with an eye on future profits rather than as gifts for their children and grandchildren. Some of these speculators purchased "country born" children from traders or fellow slaveholders. Others fancied young "outlanders" straight off the *Elizabeth* or the *Dembia* or any number of slave ships that carried names painfully ironic for the black souls they harbored—*Shepherd, Providence, Fortune, Hope.*

I bought 4 boys and 2 girls—their ages near as I can judge Sancho = 9 years old, Peter = 7, Brutus = 7, Harry = 6, Belinda = 10, Priscilla = 10, for £600.

This account book entry was made by wealthy South Carolina planter Elias

Ball II in the summer of 1756. He had taken advantage of a sale of people from the *Hare*. The ship had left Sierra Leone with 170 Africans and docked at Charleston with about 110 (many of them children).

Elias Ball II "seemed to prefer buying children," wrote his great-great-great-great-great-grandson Edward Ball.

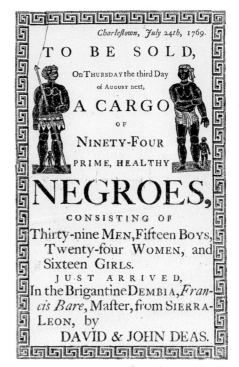

A few years after the purchase of these young ones [from the Hare*], he made this note: "[I] Bought 13 Gambius Young Negroes . . . 11 boys and 2 girls for £200 a piece which is £2600 & stake them to be about 12 years of age or there abouts."*

Edward Ball also noted that his ancestor, in his will, advised his heirs to do one of two things if they wanted to capitalize on their wealth: "either lend money at interest or 'buy Young Slaves.'"

The children Ball purchased were probably put to work right away. Generally, such children were being acquainted with work at age six or seven. Within a year or so, they were at it with forced vigor: sweeping, fetching water from the well, toting wood, hoeing potatoes, cleaning up around a cobbler's or cooper's shop, collecting trash, minding the littler ones, weeding, slinging corn to chickens, scaring birds in rice, wheat, or cornfields, and fanning dandies on verandas.

The young Jacks, Jubahs, Catos, Quacos, Phoebes, Peters, and Belindas would soon become sowers and reapers, cowherds and shepherds, stonemasons, weavers, tinsmiths, blacksmiths, cooks, coachmen, porters, maids, valets, and "mammies." Their owners hoped that one day these children would reproduce, making for another crop (to keep or to sell) of free labor for the ironworks of Pennsylvania; the tanneries of New York; the sail lofts and shipyards of Rhode Island; the cotton fields, rice fields, and indigo works of South Carolina; the planting, tilling, weeding, picking, curing, and hauling of tobacco; the raising of

A reconstructed cabin in the slave quarters at Carter's Grove plantation (near Williamsburg, Virginia), originally the property of Robert "King" Carter.

cattle and the tending of orchards and grainfields in Virginia; and the logging, hauling, stone-quarry toiling, welding, bricklaying, woodworking, cooking, cleaning, and the like to help perpetuate the comfortable lives of the Balls, the Byrds, the Carters, the Middletons, the Austins, the Washingtons, and the Jeffersons. (Some slaveholders, noted Thomas Jefferson, considered "a woman who [has] a child every two years as more valuable than the best man on the farm.")

What roles these young Africans played in the lives of the people who held them captive is understood, but the details of these children's lives are scant. For instance, Alice Morse Earle's 1899 chronicle *Child Life in Colonial Days* contains four hundred pages of facts about white children's infancy, schooling, clothing, books, toys, and more, along with reproductions of their portraits and artifacts from their lives. However, this book contains nothing about black children. Fragments, scraps—that is all that remains of their lives in colonial America.

There was Venture Smith, a prince of the tribe of Dukandarra in Guinea, whose real name was Broteer. In the mid-1730s, when Venture was about seven, he was purchased aboard a slave ship for four gallons of rum and a piece of calico, and subjected to captivity in Rhode Island.

The first of the time of living at my master's own place, I was pretty much employed in the house at carding wool and other household business. In this situation I continued for some years, after which my master put me to work out of doors. After many proofs of my faithfulness and honesty, my master began to put great confidence in me. My behavior to him had as yet been submissive and obedient. I then began to have hard tasks imposed on me. Some of these were to pound four bushels of ears of corn every night in a barrel for the poultry, or be rigorously punished. At other seasons of the year I had to card wool until a very late hour. These tasks I had to perform when I was about nine years old.

• Venture Smith (c. 1729–1805)

There was Lucy Terry Prince (c. 1725–1821), who was brought to Rhode Island as an infant. From the age of five, as the property of Ensign Ebenezer Wells, Lucy lived in Deerfield, Massachusetts. As a young woman, she wrote the first known verse by an African in North America, the ballad "Bars Fight" (1746) about a battle between Native Americans and English settlers.

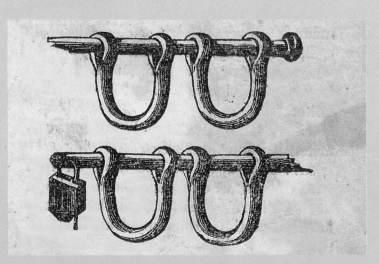

An engraving of a coffle-yoke, so called because coffles (or groups) of enslaved people were yoked about the neck, wrists, or ankles with iron devices such as the one above and then transported from place to place.

The first object which saluted my eyes when I arrived on the coast was the sea, and a slave ship, which was then riding at anchor, and waiting for its cargo. These filled me with astonishment, which was soon converted into terror when I was carried on board. I was immediately handled and tossed up to see if I were sound by some of the crew. . . . When I looked round the ship too and saw a large furnace or copper boiling, and a multitude of black people of every description chained together, every one of their countenances expressing dejection and sorrow, I no longer doubted of my fate; and, quite overpowered with horror and anguish, I fell motionless on the deck and fainted. When I recovered a little I found some black people about me, who I believed were some of those who brought me on board, and had been receiving their pay. . . . I asked them if we were not to be eaten by those white men with horrible looks, red faces, and loose hair. They told me I was not. . . .

The stench of the hold while we were on the coast was so intolerably loathsome, that it was dangerous to remain there for any time, and some of us had been permitted to stay on the deck for the fresh air; but now that the whole ship's cargo were confined together, it became absolutely pestilential. The closeness of the place, and the heat of the climate, added to the number in the ship, which was so crowded that each had scarcely room to turn himself, almost suffocated us. This produced copious perspirations, so that the air soon became unfit for respiration . . . and brought on a sickness among the slaves, of which many died. . . . This wretched situation was again aggravated by the galling of the chains . . . and the filth of the necessary tubs, into which the children often fell, and were almost suffocated.

• Olaudah Equiano (c. 1745–1797)

About a year before Lucy penned "Bars Fight," Olaudah Equiano (c. 1745–1797) was born in an Igbo village in present-day Nigeria. At about age eleven, along with his sister, Olaudah was kidnapped and eventually shipped to Barbados. After two weeks there the boy endured another ocean journey, at the end of which he became the property of a Virginia planter who put him to work "weeding grass and gathering stones." And there was a Fulani girl from Senegal kidnapped around age seven and brought to Boston in mid-July 1761 aboard a schooner named *Phillis*—the name the child then bore.

Venture, Lucy, Olaudah, Phillis—all wrenched from family at an early age, all forced to adapt to an alien world and way of life alone. Yet there were so many, at the time, who did not think these children felt pain, that these children would long for their families, their friends, their native ways. Many concurred with what Thomas Jefferson would one day write about black people: "Their griefs are transient."

PHILLIS WHEATLEY

Servant to Mr John Wheatley of Boston.

This portrait of Phillis Wheatley (1753–1784) is based on the engraving of the Boston bond-servant Scipio Moorhead, whom Phillis celebrated in her poem "To S.M. a Young African Painter, on Seeing His Works." Left: Phillis's poem, "To the University of Cambridge, in New England," was composed in 1767, when she was about fourteen. According to the Boston tailor John Wheatley (whose wife had purchased the child), Phillis mastered the English language sixteen months after her arrival in America, and later set her mind on learning Latin.

21

Where children and parents were suffering bondage together, mothers and fathers did what they could to protect their sons and daughters from too great a savaging. More than a few so loved their children that they sneaked visits to a child sold away but not far. More than a few so loved their children to the perilous point that they took them along when they attempted to escape. Take Lucy of South Carolina: In the spring of 1749, this woman fled captivity with one child in the womb and another on the hip. In many cases an escape attempt was triggered by news (or suspicion) of impending separation of families through hiring out or sale.

"Who buys me must buy my son too," a bold cooper shouted as he and his fifteen-year-old son were up for resale at a North Carolina auction in 1739. Whether this father and son were purchased by the same person is unknown, but many children had two or more owners by the time they were sixteen.

JULY 5th, 1766, Ran away from the subscriber, on Horse-Savannah. Two Negroes, father and son, both named *Bristol*; the father aged about 46, and the son 13 years: They were bought at vendue from the estate of Mr. *John Raven*; carried off with them a large bundle of cloaths, and were seen going towards *John's-Island*, where they are well known, and supposed to be harboured by their relations, having lived on Mr. *Raven's* plantation there. The father is a good fisherman. A reward of £. 10 will be paid to any person, who will apprehend and deliver them to the warden of the work-house, in *Charles-Town*, or to Mr. *John Cooper*, at *Rantowle's*-Bridge. JOHN HALY.

This item is from the July 28–August 4, 1766, edition of the *South Carolina Gazette*.

ELOP'D from the subscriber the 6th instant *(August)*, a negro boy named JACK, he is about 12 years of age, had on when he went away an oznabrug shirt and green pair of breeches, and is supposed to be harboured by his father *Cupid*, belonging to *Thomas Wright*, Esq; in *Charles-Town*. Whoever delivers the said negro to me or the warden of the work-house in *Charles-Town*, shall receive FORTY SHILLINGS reward. JOHN LAMPERT.

This item is from the August 16–August 23, 1760, edition of the *South Carolina Gazette*.

And some young people had the gumption to spirit away to their parents. Such a plucky child was Esther, the property of the Charleston merchant Robert Pringle. In 1740 Pringle sold Esther because he was fed up with her "practice of [going] frequently to her Father and Mother," who were in captivity on a plantation about twenty miles from Charleston.

Some "men-boys" (age fourteen to eighteen) and "women-girls" (age thirteen to sixteen), as the colonists called them, ran away not to a parent but to freedom, perhaps to one of the maroon settlements, such as Fort Mose (established 1738) in St. Augustine, Florida (then a Spanish possession).

I was born in Princeton (New Jersey) in the year 1769 or '70, and was born, as was my mother (who was of African descent) in bondage; although my father . . . was not only a pure white blooded Englishman, but a gentleman of considerable eminence—I had no brothers and but one sister, who was three years older than myself; but of her, as of my mother, I have but a faint recollection, as I in my infancy was included in the patrimonial portion of my master's oldest daughter, on her marriage to a Mr. John Voorhis, by birth a German. When but four years of age I was conveyed by my master to Georgetown . . . to which place he removed with his family, and never have I since been enabled to learn the fate of my poor mother or sister. . . .

At the age of 14 or 15, my master apprenticed me to a shoemaker, to obtain if possible a knowledge of the art; but making but little proficiency, he again took me upon his plantation, where my time was mostly employed in gardening until about the age of nineteen.

• Robert Voorhis (c. 1769–?)

Occasionally, children were freed upon the death of their owners. And sometimes these owners were the children's biological fathers. In his last will and testament, dated February 19, 1761, Thomas Hadden of Scarsdale, New York, stated that "at my death all my negroes are to be free," and he requested that all the children be apprenticed to a trade and taught to read. Furthermore, as concerned the black children he had fathered, Hadden, who owned a 150-acre farm, decreed the following:

I leave to my negro children, their bedding and clothes, and to my wench Rose, £25. To my negro boys Francis and Robert £20 each. . . . My executors are to sell 10 sheep which my two oldest negro boys have, and put the money at interest for them.

View of Mount Vernon from the Northeast (c. 1792) attributed to Edward Savage. When, in 1761, George Washington inherited this estate near Alexandria, Virginia, it comprised about 2,000 acres. At the time of Washington's death (1799), the estate had expanded to about 8,000 acres, with five large farms. In his will, Washington freed about 123 of the 300 people in captivity at Mount Vernon.

Some slaveholders were far from generous toward their enslaved children. Consider the case of Benjamin Steymets, who lived in the Kings County town of Gravesend (now part of Brooklyn, New York). In May 1750 Steymets—"being very sick"— willed his estate to his white wife, Sarah, and their eight children, with the following directive about his black family:

> *My negro woman "Cate" and my 2 negro children are to be sold by my executors to pay debts.*

Other children were saved from bondage through purchase by a parent, friend, or other acquaintance. This was the case with young Mary and John Ashby of Williamsburg, Virginia. From his work as a carpenter and sometime messenger, their

A bill of sale, dated October 8, 1772, for a boy named James who purchased himself for five shillings from Robert Pleasants of Henrico County, Virginia.

father, the former indentured servant Matthew Ashby (son of a black man and a white indentured servant) came up with the money to buy his children and his wife, Ann, from the bricklayer Samuel Spurr in 1769. Matthew Ashby paid 150 pounds sterling for his family—no small sum. At the time, a white nonslaveholding family of four in the South had, on average, an annual household income of about 50 pounds. (And, technically, Matthew Ashby's wife and children were his slaves until his petition to free them was granted.)

What was it like to be a free black child in colonial America?

Most free black families were far from well-to-do. Mere survival was a struggle. The children had to work on the family farm, at Papa's blacksmith, carpentry, or carriage shop, or at Mama's laundry, sewing, or catering business.

Many children were "bound out" by their parents—as house servants, as field hands, and as apprentices to cartwrights, tanners, tailors, shoemakers, printers, and other tradespeople. The indenture might begin as early as age seven and last until age seventeen or longer. Often room and board was the payment. Fortunate was the child bound to a fairly decent person, but many were not so lucky: Sometimes there was little difference between being bound out and being in bondage.

Not all free black children in colonial America lived impoverished lives. The most well-known example is Maryland's Benjamin Banneker (1731–1806). He grew up relatively unfettered; got his mind primed at a nearby one-room Quaker

The Quaker Anthony Benezet of Philadelphia, Pennsylvania, drawn here with two of his students, was an ardent abolitionist and advocate of education of blacks.

school; was a whiz kid in math; had time to ponder the bees, the seasons, the stars; and could visit with the woman who had taught him to read and write, his English grandmother, the once-indentured servant Molly Welsh. Molly had married a man once her slave: Bannka, son of a Senegalese chieftain, whose name evolved into Banneker and became the family's surname.

Molly and Bannka's daughter Mary married an African freedman named Robert, who decided to take Banneker as his last name. Together, Mary and Robert built a rich farm on which they raised four children. Their firstborn and only son was Benjamin, who grew up to make a clock from the mere observation of a pocket watch; to assist with the mapping out of Washington, D.C.; to produce several prized almanacs; and, in cogent correspondence, to challenge Thomas Jefferson on his skewed racial views.

The outcry of blacks and whites (many of them Quakers) against slavery had little effect. In the early 1770s there were about 460,000 enslaved children, women, and men in the thirteen colonies (total population: about 2.2 million). However, as restless colonists became determined to cast off British rule, a multitude of enslaved adults hoped that they and their children would soon be free. After all, many Patriots claimed to abhor slavery: They deemed it a sin and a shame, an undue burden.

Several thousand blacks (free, freed, enslaved) fought for the new nation, and there were some young folks among the black Patriots. Most notable was Philadelphia's future entrepreneur, philanthropist, and abolitionist, the free-born James Forten (1766–1842), who attended the school started by the Quaker

THE JERSEY PRISON-SHIP.

Anthony Benezet and did odd jobs at the sail-making company he would one day own. In 1781 young James cast off as a powder boy aboard the *Royal Louis*, leaving behind his sister and widowed mother. His service included six month's captivity aboard Great Britain's foulest prison ship, the *Jersey*.

When he was once again free, James expected there to be broad liberty granted every black soul in the breakaway republic behind which he and other blacks had rallied. Instead, in this wonderful-terrible, conflicted, contradictory new nation, slavery would grow.

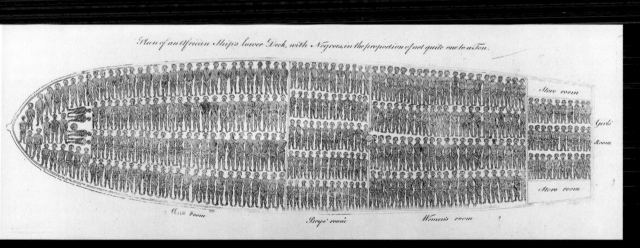

Top: An engraving of the British ship on which the young James Forten was held captive during the American Revolution. Above: A late eighteenth-century engraving of a proposed slave ship's lower deck with separate storage compartments for men, women, girls, and boys.

Slaves

Two unidentified
children photograph
(c. 1864) in
or near Beaufort,
South Carolina, by
Hubbard and Mix.

PART II

Longing for the Jubilee

When the American Revolution was over (1783), some black people—children among them—spirited themselves away to Native American strongholds in Florida and elsewhere. Others shipped out with Loyalists and British forces, expecting a better life in Canada, Nova Scotia, or England. (Sadly, some of them were then sold into slavery in the West Indies.)

The free blacks who remained in the United States did so because it was home and they had hopes for the nation. Relatively few embraced the black- and white-sponsored back-to-Africa endeavors that promised a better life in Liberia or Sierra Leone.

As for the majority of Africans in the United States, they were still enslaved and had no choice but to stay. By 1790, the year of the first Federal census, in the states that then made up the nation, there were close to 760,000 blacks (a little less than 20 percent of the total population), with about 700,000 of them in bondage. Through births and importation (most from Africa, some from the West Indies), the number of enslaved people would swell to nearly four million by 1860, with about 1.7 million of them girls and boys under the age of fifteen.

During this time, the new country expanded to thirty-six states, growing southward and westward through purchase, through conquest, through greed. More fields, forests, and rivers meant more opportunities for profit: timber, fur and hides, rice and other grains, livestock and game, and the crop that became the South's king, cotton. And it was cotton more than any other crop that made so many in the ruling class deem slavery a necessity for the wealth they desired.

By the mid-nineteenth century slavery had been completely abolished in the Northern states (with Vermont the first in 1777 and New Jersey the last in 1846). The North, however, was not an absolute safe haven for blacks. The North had its share of laws and customs that allowed free blacks only limited liberty. Black people were denied full U.S. citizenship until 1868, when the Fourteenth Amendment to the Constitution was ratified.

A nation within a nation thus was born. Among Africa's people in America, ethnic differences and ancient hostilities faded. Cultures merged. The sons and daughters and the grandchildren and the great-grandchildren of the Asante, Fulani, Kwi, Mandinka, Temne, and other African peoples metamorphosed into one people—*E Pluribus Unum*, indeed. Skin color now determined a person's life chances and circumstances—determined that a child would be at worst brutalized, at best marginalized. And the children yearned for relief.

Marbles, ring games, hide-the-switch, make-pretend gallops on a stick . . . little Cora did not have a porcelain dolly like her owner's daughter, but she might have had a corncob doll or one of patched rags or flour sackcloth. Little Isom might have had marbles made of sun-baked clay, and Jake's daddy may have whittled him a whistle. All three would have had an imagination big enough to conjure piney woods or city street adventures.

In precious let-loose times, right along with the adults, children danced—learning reels or do-si-dos or moves from a place they could never call home but a place that perhaps called to their souls: Africa. They caught on to the hambone act, making music—flesh upon flesh slap-pat-clap—with hands and limbs that, legally, did not belong to them.

Some learned how to "shake that gourd," "make a good chord" on the "banjer," or "hit a right lick" on a cut of rawhide stretched across one end of a hollowed-out

Above: These clay marbles, which date to the late eighteenth century, were unearthed in a root cellar in the slave quarters at Carter's Grove plantation near Williamsburg, Virginia. Below: Evidence suggests that this doll (c. 1850) belonged to an enslaved child. The doll was found in the wall of an attic on the Bonnehan plantation near Durham, North Carolina.

Us made play houses under the big oak trees. Us raked up big piles of leaves for beds, and made rag-dolls . . . and dresses and hats out of leaves pinned together with pine straws. Then us played run and ketch games us made up.

• Manda Boggan, once enslaved in Mississippi

31

The Banjo Lesson (1893) by Henry Ossawa Tanner. Though created after slavery was abolished, this painting conveys the love so many children received from their elders: love often expressed through the passing on of skills and traditions, such as playing the "banjer," as some called this stringed instrument that originated in Africa.

log. (Laws prohibiting blacks from playing the drum—through which they could possibly communicate about uprisings—were not universal.)

There was play across the color line, and in most cases the white children had the upper hand. Candis Goodwin of Virginia recalled that when the game was "Injuns an' soldiers," the black boys had to be the Native Americans (the "bad guys" in most white minds of the time), and had to let themselves get "shot," fall dead, and then suffer a mock scalping.

"Marse, will you give me a white man's chance?" a boy asked when he played with his owner's son, Hilary Herbert. In his memoirs, Herbert maintained that he did allow this black boy "a white man's chance" in their games. Herbert, who grew up to be a lawyer, congressional representative, and secretary of the navy, summed up the relationship: "We were friends." Whether or not the black boy felt the same way is not known.

Of course, recreation was a very small part of a young slave's life. Late in life, many former slaves could not summon up any memory of childhood fun and games at all. Work was all that came to mind.

My mama died when I was two years old and my aunty raised me. She started me out washing dishes when I was four years old and when I was six she was learning me how to cook. While the other hands was working in the field I carried water. We had to cook out in the yard on an old skillet and lid, so you see I had to tote brush and bark and roll up little logs such as I could to keep the fire from one time of cooking to the other. . . . When I got to be seven years old I was cutting sprouts almost like a man and when I was eight I could pick one hundred pounds of cotton. When it rained and we could not go to the field my aunty had me spinning thread to make socks and cloth, then I had to card the bats and make the rolls to spin.

• Mary Island who grew up in Union Parish, Louisiana

Work that was not backbreaking could still burden. Along with minding the table, fanning the flies, and gathering dung for fires, John Smith, who grew up in Virginia, remembered that children under twelve might also be tasked with "scratchin' Master's head so he could sleep in the evenings, an' washin' Missus' feet at night, 'fore she went to bed."

We didn't have hardly any clothes and most of the time they was just rags. We went barefoot until it got real cold. Our feet would crack open from the cold and bleed. We would sit down bawl and cry because it hurt so. Mother made moccasins for our feet from old pants. Late in the fall master would go to Hannibal or Palmyra and bring us shoes and clothes. We got those things only once a year. I had to wear the young master's overalls for underwear and linseys for a dress.

• Emma Knight, who, along with her father, mother, and two sisters, was enslaved on a small farm in Missouri

Nursemaid and Her Charge
(c. 1855)

When there wasn't work to worry over, children were faced with serious obstacles just to stay alive: tetanus, lockjaw, fevers, malnutrition, wretched shelter. "They died in droves," lamented historian John W. Blassingame. Many who survived infancy were saddled with stunted growth, rickets, and other ailments.

As in the colonial era, many enslaved children lived with the fear of separation from their families. Mama might be rented out, Papa might be rented out, a child might be rented out. The entire family might be sold—miles, counties, states away from one another.

Violence also marred many young lives. Children

Aunt Viney took care of us. She had a big old horn what she blowed when it was time for us to eat. . . . There was a great long trough what went plum 'cross the yard, and that was whar us et.

For dinner, us had peas or some other sort of veg'tables, and corn bread. Aunt Viney crumbled up that bread in the trough and poured the veg'tables and pot-licker over it. Then, she blowed the horn and chillun come a-runnin' from evvy which away. . . . At nights, she crumbled the corn bread in the trough and poured buttermilk over it. Us never had nothin' but corn bread and buttermilk, at night.

• Robert Shepherd. Like Robert, many very young children on large plantations were taken care of by an elderly woman while their parents labored.

were beaten by owners, overseers, and drivers: for falling asleep while rocking little "Marse" in his cradle, for spilling the chamber pot, for not picking enough cotton. They were kicked, swatted, slapped, paddled, and lashed, sometimes just because they were little and black.

A mid-nineteenth-century engraving of a long, thick, tightly plaited whip known as a cart-whip.

Rebecca Grant, who served a South Carolinian ("polishing her brass andirons and scrubbing her floors"), recounted being beaten, at age eight, with "a raw cowhide strap, 'bout two feet long," for not addressing her Mistress's three- or four-year-old son as Marse Henry.

Seeing a parent brutalized was not uncommon. Josiah Henson (1789–1883), born in Maryland, recalled that his first memory of his father was "with his head bloody" and with his "back lacerated" from one hundred stripes, and with his right ear "cut off close to his head." Allen Wilson of Virginia recalled seeing the overseer "take my dear mother; strip her clothes off down to her waist; tie her to a ole peach

The child prodigy Thomas Greene Bethune Wiggins (1849-1908), enslaved in Columbus, Georgia, was severely exploited by his owner, who made hundreds of thousands of dollars from the boy's concerts.

tree . . . right behind the house whar we lived in and give her 9 and 30 with his cowhide."

"Us could track him the next day by the blood stains," said Hannah Chapman, who was living in Simpson County, Mississippi, when interviewed in the 1930s. Hannah was speaking of her father, who had been sold to a nearby planter. As often as he could, Hannah's father slipped back to his family's cottage at night—"Us would gather 'round him and crawl up in his lap, tickled slap to death"—risking a beating if his owner caught him with his family.

Where there was enough food, tolerable clothing, no beatings, and time to play, there was still bondage, and so many casual cruelties. Katie Sutton remembered Mistress telling her that white children were brought to their mothers by a stork "but that the slave children were all hatched out from buzzards' eggs."

[Missus] kept me right with her most of the time, an' when mealtime come she put me under the table an' I ate out of her hand. She'd put a piece of meat into a biscuit an' hand it down to me. Then, she say, "When that been finished, holler up after some more, Ike." But she allus warn me not to holler if there been company to dinner. She'd say, "Jes' put your hand on my knee an' then I'll know you is ready."

• Ike Simpson, who also recalled that as a child, he "slept by Missus' bed"

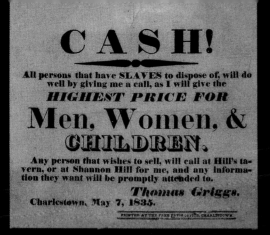

Psychological and physical torment. Anger. Fear. How did the children cope?

Parents did whatever they could to help their little ones have a life and to raise them right, whether it was preparing elderberry leaves for rashes or cornshuck tea for measles, or singing lullabies, or sneaking treats from the Big House pantry, or standing between their child and the lash, or smacking a child for misbehaving so the overseer would not administer a worse beating, or chastising a child for telling a white person about the secret talks and secret church in the quarters (in many places slaves were forbidden to assemble without the presence of a white person). Not every parent, of course, was a model, a saint, or even sane. The testament of hope is that so many were.

There were also Grandpappies and Auntie Celias and Uncle Virgils (related by blood and not) who saved children from total desolation. Frank Bell, who was

Above: An advertisement attesting to the fact that after the importation of slaves was abolished in 1808, the price of slaves went up. Left: *Slave Trader* (1853) by Lewis Miller, who witnessed a coffle of people being marched from Staunton, Virginia, to Tennessee. The robust production of short staple cotton in Alabama, Mississippi, Tennessee, and East Texas led a lot of landowners in the Upper South to start new or additional farms and plantations in the West.

Cabins made of a mixture of oyster shells, lime, sand, and water (known as "tabby") on the Kingsley plantation on St. Georges Island in Florida. Many children, not serving in the Big House, rarely had a belly full. On a large plantation, children ate whatever could be made of the rations: usually corn, molasses, lard, cured meats (beef, pork, or fish). If captives were allowed to have a garden, there would be root vegetables and beans and some kind of green in some meals.

held in Virginia, had mostly fuzzy memories of his grandfather, but crystal clear was the day when the old man "picked me up and rid me 'cross his foot with his knee crossed, holding onto my hands, and riding me up and down." After a while the old man said, "Son, I sho hope you never have to go through the things your ole grandpa done been through." These words were a thousand hugs.

For some children there was no balm. Some took the horror of bondage out on themselves, becoming resigned to seeing themselves as nothing more than slaves: There are stories of black children playing slave auction. Some children took it out on weaker ones: Jacob Stroyer recalled the bully Gilbert, who forced little ones into the woods, where he made them strip and then whipped them, cruelly mimicking what he had observed white people do.

Others resisted. Twelve-year-old Charity, for example, put poison in the coffee of the people who held her captive in Louisville, Kentucky. William Drew Robeson (1845–1918) took flight. He was about fifteen when he fled North Carolina and pushed on to Pennsylvania, eventually getting a college education and then becoming a minister in New Jersey (and later, father of the famous entertainer and activist Paul Robeson).

Learning to read was yet another act of resistance. There was the Maryland lad Fred Bailey who, in the 1820s, was taught his ABCs by his mistress. After her husband compelled her to stop the lessons, the boy persevered on the sly by getting white lads in the neighborhood to teach him. Then, when he was about thirteen years old, the boy procured a copy of *The Columbian Orator*, an anthology of writings "calculated to improve youth and others in the ornamental and useful art of eloquence." Especially affecting to him were the selections that denounced slavery. "Every opportunity I got, I used to read this book."

With reading under his belt, Fred then took on writing. "As I

Drawing of Anna Maria Weems (1840–?), who at age fifteen, with the help of Underground Railroad agents, escaped captivity in Rockville, Maryland, dressed in male attire and going by the name Joe Wright. She arrived in Philadelphia on Thanksgiving Day 1855.

might have occasion to write my own pass," he later wrote. (And definitely, if he hoped to escape one day, he would want to be able to forge a pass.) After learning to write four letters, he tricked some white boys into teaching him the rest. "During this time my copy-book was the board fence, brick wall, and pavement; my pen and ink was a lump of chalk." At one point he began making use of his owner's son's used notebooks "writing in the spaces left in Master Thomas's copy-book, copying what he had written." There came a day when young Fred could "write a hand very similar to that of Master Thomas,"

A spread from Frederick Douglass's own copy of *The Columbian Orator*, which he purchased with money he earned as a "bootblack," as shoe shine boys were once called.

as he recalled decades later—by which time he had long since liberated himself and changed his name to Frederick Douglass (1818–1895).

Frederick Douglass's ingenuity was matched and surpassed by many. Another quick spirit was John Sella Martin, an errand boy for a hotel in Columbus, Georgia. He champed many a white boy at marbles and often traded the boys back their marbles for reading lessons.

The extent to which children had to resort to cunning to learn to read and write depended on the place of their captivity and the dispositions of those who held them in bondage. Some states had laws prohibiting the instruction of the enslaved. Where laws did not exist, white public opinion often made it seem as if they did. Offenders were sometimes severely punished. Many former slaves recalled that lobbing off the first joint of a forefinger was one such punishment.

The boy in this daguerreotype (c. 1850) was the property of the wealthy Bunker family in Mobile, Alabama.

Well, daughter, when I was mighty young, just about your age, I used to steal away under a big oak tree and I tried to learn my alphabets so that I could learn to read my Bible. But one day the overseer caught me and he drug me out on the plantation and he called out for all the field hands. And he turned to 'em and said, "Let this be a lesson to all of you darkies. You ain't got no right to learn to read!" And then daughter, he whooped me, and he whooped me, and he whooped me. And daughter, as if that wasn't enough, he turned around and he burned my eyes out! . . . .

"Don't you cry for me now, daughter. . . . I want you to promise me one thing. Promise me that you gonna pick up every book you can and you gonna read it from cover to cover. . . . Promise me that you gonna go all the way through school, as far as you can. And one more thing, I want you to promise me that you gonna tell all the children my story."

• This was what five- or six-year-old Tonea Stewart's "Papa Dallas" told her one day as they sat on the front porch of their home in Mississippi. Aware that he was blind and curious about the "ugly scars around his eyes," young Tonea had asked her Papa Dallas what had happened to his eyes.

Education was a treasure for the majority of free black children as well. Most of these children lived in the Northeast, the overwhelming majority in Pennsylvania, New York, and Massachusetts. Their parents were artisans, blacksmiths, barbers, carters, caterers, farmers, laborers, and servants. No matter where they lived, parents, in case after case, regarded schooling as vital as food, shelter, and clothing: as the means to get ahead.

Many youngsters in New York had celebrated in 1787 when the New York Manumission Society launched the African Free School project as had young Bostonians in 1798 when the African School opened in the home of Primus Hall. The nineteenth century saw these schools multiply and expand.

Hallelujahs ballooned over several Quaker schools up and running in New Jersey by 1800; over the school Absalom Jones opened in the basement of his Philadelphia church, St. Thomas (1804); over the Bell School in Washington, D.C. (1807); over the schools for black girls started by Roman Catholic orders in the 1830s in Baltimore, Nashville, and New Orleans; and over those schools Jeremiah Burke Sanderson started in the 1850s in Oakland, San Francisco, Sacramento, and Stockton, California.

Top: An engraving of Manhattan's African Free School #2, based on a drawing by one of its students, future professional artist Patrick Henry Reason (1816–1898). Bottom: Samplers such as this one were once a common exercise for young girls in American schools.

F rom a Ten-Year-Old

Dear Sir,—This is to inform you that I have two cousins in slavery who are entitled to their freedom. They have done everything that the will requires and now they won't let them go. They talk of selling them down the river. If this was your case what would you do? Please give me your advice.

From a Sixteen-Year-Old

Let us look back and see the state in which the Britons and the Saxons and Germans lived. They had no learning and had not a knowledge of letters. But now look, some of them are our first men. Look at king Alfred and see what a great man he was. He at one time did not know his a, b, c, but before his death he commanded armies and nations. He was never discouraged but always looked forward and studied the harder. I think if the colored people study like king Alfred they will soon do away the evil of slavery. I can't see how Americans can call this a land of freedom where so much slavery is.

• Two of the surviving responses to the question "What do you think *most* about?" posed, in 1834, to young Cincinnatans attending schools started and maintained by blacks

Few schools established for white children admitted blacks; those that did often proved to be toxic environments. "I get along pretty well, but father, Miss Tracy does not allow me to go into the room with the other scholars because I am colored." This from tearful nine-year-old Rosetta to her father, Frederick Douglass, in the fall of 1848. He had asked how she got along at Seward Seminary in Rochester, New York, where the Douglasses lived. He was outraged that his daughter was subjected to

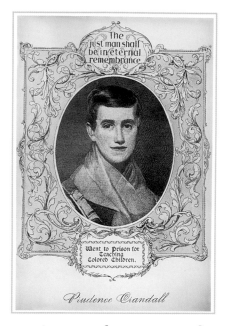

The
just man shall
be in eternal
remembrance

Went to prison for
Teaching
Colored Children.

Prudence Crandall

"prison-like solitary confinement" as he put it, especially since the principal, Miss Tracy, was an abolitionist.

Generally, members of the small black middle class were vigilant about not raising self-centered souls. Their children were groomed not only for individual success but also to help uplift the race. Such children grew up with antislavery alphabet books and broadsides. They contributed money to campaigns to buy men, women, and children out of bondage. They joined youth divisions of antislavery societies. They kept hush-hush about family members and family friends who were agents for the Underground Railroad.

Among these young heroes was the Bostonian (and future historian) William Cooper Nell (1816–1874), a sterling student and leader in the Juvenile Garrison Independent Society. In New York City there was future minister and activist Henry Highland Garnet (1815–1882), whose family escaped bondage in Maryland when he was nine. He attended African Free School #2, as did his good friend, the future scholar Alexander Crummell (1819–1898), whose father, Boston Crummell, helped launch the first black newspaper, *Freedom's Journal* (1827).

At age fourteen Alexander Crummell, who proclaimed the Declaration of Independence "a perfect mockery," was among the youth who

THE
SLAVE'S FRIEND.

Vol. II. No. II.   Whole No. 14.

DEC. INDEPEN.   BIBLE

FOR SALE AT THE ANTI-SLAVERY OFFICE,
Corner of Nassau and Spruce sts., New-York.

☞ *Price*—One cent single; 10 cts. a dozen; 80 cts. per
hundred; $6.60 per thousand

Top: PrudenceCrandall was driven out of Canterbury, Connecticut, in the mid-1830s for opening a boarding school for black girls. Bottom: The cover of an 1837 edition of *The Slave's Friend* (1836–1838), an illustrated monthly magazine intended to educate free children about the evils of slavery and to get them involved in the antislavery movement.

Three Sisters of the Coplan Family (1854) by William Matthew Prior. The girls in the painting are Eliza, Nellie, and Margaret Coplan, members of a middle-class family in Boston.

Wednesday, May 24, 1854 . . . . How bright and beautiful are these May mornings! The air is so pure and balmy, the trees are in full blossom, and the little birds sing sweetly. I stand by the window listening to their music, but suddenly remember that I have an Arithmetic lesson which employs me until breakfast; then to school, recited my lessons, and commenced my journal. After dinner practiced a music lesson, did some sewing, and then took a pleasant walk by the water. I stood for some time admiring the waves as they rose and fell, sparkling in the sun, and could not help envying a party of boys who were enjoying themselves in a sailing boat. On my way home, I stopped at Mrs. Putnam's and commenced reading "Hard Times," a new story by Dickens.

• Charlotte Forten (1837–1914), granddaughter of Revolutionary War hero James Forten, whose successful sail-making business in Philadelphia enabled his children and grandchildren to live relatively privileged lives

Many free children were aware that Africans were being smuggled into the United States long after the nation abolished the importation of slaves in 1808. When this image appeared in the early 1880s in *The Graphic*, it carried the caption: "The African Slave-Trade—Slaves Taken from a Dhow Captured by H.M.S. *Undine*."

vowed never to celebrate the Fourth of July until slavery was abolished nation-wide. "For years our society met on that day," he later recalled, "and the time was devoted to planning schemes for the freeing and upbuilding our race. The other resolve which was made was, that when we had educated ourselves we should go South, start an insurrection and free our brethren in bondage."

Just as in the South, these children also had their problems. As a Crummell biographer noted, "The black schoolchildren, who were jeered in the streets and pelted with stones, often had to be escorted to and from school by their parents." Not all were cowed—not future Rhode Island restaurant owner and civil rights activist George T. Downing (1819–1903). Young George, it was said, "would bold-ly lead colored boys into chasing white ones from the street." This same George

D̲ear Uncle,

I am very pleased to have it in my power to write. It is the first time and I hope you will bear with me. . . . I mean to try this next year to improve both in my music and my writing. . . . I mean to be in the year very industrious and try to please every-body and I hope I shall keep my resolution.

• A letter dated December 25, 1822, from six-going-on seven-year-old Euphemia Toussaint to her uncle and adoptive father Pierre Toussaint. Euphemia had recently started taking classes with Mrs. Ruckels, a white woman who taught a handful of students in the rooms she rented in the Toussaint house in lower Manhattan.

Above: Euphemia Toussaint (c. 1820)

helped his father hide escapees from slavery in the cellar of their famous restaurant in lower Manhattan.

Life for free children was not all school and protests. There were those who had their picnics and frolics, their music lessons, pastimes, and treats. But there were those who had no niceties at all. They lived in death trap city slums, on threadbare farms near pitiful towns, and in ramshackle cabins and lean-tos in wilderness America. Yet not all of these poor children were devoid of hope and a desire to make something of themselves. There was, for one, Elleanor Eldridge (1785–1862) of Warwick, Rhode Island. She was ten when her mother died, leaving her father with nine children to raise. For twenty-five cents a week, she went to work for a family for which her mother had worked as a laundress. Elleanor quickly picked up many other skills, including spinning and weaving. As a woman, she earned a reputation as a savvy entrepreneur, running a home remodeling business for a time and investing in real estate.

Whatever their status, many children kept up with current events, especially those that affected black life for better or for worse. They eavesdropped on grown folks' talk. Those who could read shared with others what they gleaned from newspapers and magazines. Many children learned a great deal from those whites who talked freely around blacks, assuming they would not understand.

Some children knew about the work of Frederick Douglass, William Lloyd Garrison, Wendell Phillips, and other abolitionists. They heard about Nat Turner's rebellion in Virginia, about John Brown's raid on Harpers Ferry, and about the firing on Fort Sumter, in mid-April 1861, which catapulted the nation into a civil war. Loads of little souls were on tiptoe when they heard that President Lincoln was soon to issue the Emancipation Proclamation, which, on January 1, 1863—"the Day of Jubilee"— freed millions of children, their parents, and other elders held in "Rebel" territory.

As the Civil War waged, children had much cause for rejoicing and much cause for tears. Children learned of battles, bayonets, and blood firsthand. They were with Confederate and Union soldiers and sailors, serving by choice or force: grooming horses, cooking, cleaning, foraging for supplies and provisions, being scouts, being runabouts.

A document of indenture, dated August 11, 1841, from Kent County, Delaware, for ten-year-old Rachel Trusty, who was to be a domestic servant to former Governor Jacob Stout until she was eighteen years old. At the end of Rachel's indenture, Stout was "to furnish her with two suits of clothing suitable to her condition, and also to pay said Rachel Trusty the sum of Three dollars in lieu of schooling." Rachel's father was paid one dollar up front.

Maritcha Lyons
(c. 1860)

During [my senior] year, my composition themes were usually chosen from a list of race topics; and as I wrote out of the fullness of my heart, they rarely failed to create a sensation. They were frequently read in class and my chum, Miss Lucia Tappen, a member of the famous abolition family, was reader for me. My sketches of the riots of 63; the Underground Railroad; of episodes on southern plantations; of freedmen and incidents of the Civil War, never failed to elicit comment. Sometimes the teacher would question me privately: "Is what you wrote really true, or have you been letting loose your imagination?" My reply was invariably: "The half has never been told."

• Maritcha Lyons (1848–1929) was born in New York City. When her family's home was looted during the Draft Riots of 1863, her family relocated to Providence, Rhode Island. There, after her mother's lawsuit, Maritcha became the first black student to attend the local high school. Maritcha eventually became a teacher and, in the 1920s, the first black woman assistant principal in New York City.

One young hero for the Union was Georgia-born Susie King (1848–1912). She was among a crowd liberated by Union troops in April 1862 and eventually resettled in Camp Saxton in Beaufort, South Carolina. There, at age fourteen, Susie served as laundress and clerk, and then, as nurse, working for a time with the founder of the American Red Cross, Clara Barton.

Some slaveholders, to flee the war, pulled up stakes and headed West (many to Texas), taking only the strongest slaves, leaving the children behind. Children also lost fathers when slaveholders forced male slaves to serve in the Confederate Army or Navy. Many children died when their owners cut off their food supply or from illnesses or from many other causes.

Top: James Henry Brooks, nicknamed "Jim Limber," who lived for a time with Jefferson Davis and his family in the Confederate White House in Richmond, Virginia. Bottom: The boy in this photograph may have belonged to the man on the left, 2nd Lt. James B. Washington, a Confederate soldier taken prisoner on May 31, 1862. The man on the right, 2nd Lt. George Armstrong Custer, with the Union army, later made a name for himself making war on Native Americans.

Good Friday, 1861, outside the orphanage for black children at 42nd Street and Fifth Avenue in Manhattan. During the Civil War, in mid-July 1863, a mob attacked the orphanage, vandalized and looted it, and then set it on fire. Fortunately, the staff and the children (more than two hundred, all under age twelve) escaped. This occurred on day one of four days of beatings, murders, vandalism, and arson known as the New York City Draft Riots. As historian Charles M. Christian explained, "these riots actually stemmed from the widespread belief among whites, especially the Irish, that they were being forced to fight for blacks whose freedom would then threaten their jobs." Because of the riots, hundreds of blacks left New York City, as they did in Boston, Chicago, Cleveland, Detriot, and other northern cities after working-class whites reacted similarly to the draft.

Black children in the South had a certain distrust of the Union soldiers who were moving through the land. To keep the children from running off, slave-holders told them horrible tales, such as describing the soldiers as black-flesh-eating monsters. Some children felt they had good reason to fear Union troops when they heard about or witnessed them pillaging plantations. Some did not know whom to trust, or if talk of freedom was true. Some did not know what they would do if the war was ever over. And there were those too young to under-stand what was going on.

One of the first things that I remembers was my pappy waking me up in the middle of the night, dressing me in the dark, all the time telling me to keep quiet. One of the twins hollered some, and Pappy put his hand over its mouth to keep it quiet.

After we was dressed, he went outside and peeped around for a minute, then he comed back and got us. We snook out of the house and along the woods path, Pappy toting one of the twins and holding me by the hand and Mammy carrying the other two.

I reckons that I will always remember that walk, with the bushes slapping my legs, the wind sighing in the trees, and the hoot owls and whippoorwills hollering at each other from the big trees. I was half asleep and scared stiff, but in a little while we pass the plum thicket and there am the mules and wagon. There am the quilt in the bottom of the wagon, and on this they lays we younguns. And Pappy and Mammy gets on the board across the front and drives off down the road. . . .

We was scared of the Yankees to start with, but the more we thinks about us running away from our marsters, the scareder we gets of the Rebs. Anyhow, Pappy says that we is going to join the Yankees.

• Mary Barbour (c. 1865–?) born in McDowell County, North Carolina

A Ride for Liberty—The Fugitive Slaves (c. 1862) by Eastman Johnson. On the back of the painting the artist wrote: "A veritable incident of the Civil War seen by myself at Centerville in the morning of McClelland's advance to Manassas, March 2, 1862."

Pencil drawing (May 14, 1864) of women and children in a cabin in Spotsylvania, Virginia, by Edwin Forbes.

When General Robert E. Lee surrendered to General Ulysses S. Grant at Appomattox in April 1865 and the Civil War was, for all intents and purposes, over—and with it, slavery—some children jumped for joy while others were bewildered. Where was family? Where now was home?

Finding family was the priority for so many freedpeople—children and adults alike—who had been separated from loved ones by sale, self-purchase, or escape, before or during the war. They placed ads in newspapers. They wrote letters to government officials, to private relief organizations, to anybody they thought might be able to help. They asked people they met along the way to somewhere—anywhere—that was not the place of their enslavement. They did not have photographs. They did not always have a surname. They only had hope.

Some parents knew very well where their children were: in captivity. There were people (some former slaveholders, some not) who essentially re-enslaved children during and after the war. They called it "apprenticeship," securing the necessary paperwork to keep control of a child until he or she was twenty-one or older. Many found the pickings easy in orphanages. Others simply ignored the protests of a child's parent or other family member.

Family reunions were not the only thing freedpeople had on their minds. Education, for many, was a top priority: During Reconstruction (1863–1877) roughly three thousand schools for blacks sprang up under the auspices of the

This 1866 drawing by Alfred R. Waud depicts Union soldiers reuniting with their families in Little Rock, Arkansas.

51—Sugar Cane Plantation, La.

NEGRO NEWS-BOYS IN RICHMOND DIVIDING THEIR PROFITS.—[SKETCHED BY W. L. SHEPPARD.]

Bureau of Refugees, Freedmen, and Abandoned Lands, better known as the Freedmen's Bureau, a government agency. Schools were also formed through the efforts of individuals and religious and civic organizations.

For many children, formal education was not possible because poverty forced them to work, work, work, leaving them little time for school or anything else.

Violence was another impediment to many children's development. During Reconstruction, there were legions of crimes against black life and

Opposite page, top: A stereograph of children in a field of sugarcane in Louisiana taken in the late nineteenth century. Opposite page, bottom: An engraving by W. L. Sheppard, which appeared in the December 12, 1868, edition of *Harper's Weekly* with the caption: "Negro news-boys in Richmond dividing their profits." Above: A photograph of unidentified children in the ruins of Charleston, South Carolina, taken in the mid-1860s.

Dear Children:

I am a little black boy. I don't suppose I'll ever be white. I'm free, though. My mother is dead, my father went off with the Yankees. I lived in the camps one year with the Yankee soldiers. I used to dance around the camp for sugar and bread. Now I has a nice home with Miss Wells. She teaches me to be good and I am trying to be the best boy in the world.

I have read through the First and Second Reader and now I am in the Third Reader. I have very nice clothes with pockets in them; I eat with a fork. I used to sit on the floor and eat with my fingers, and get grease and molasses all over myself. I didn't have any manners nor anything to eat hardly. Now I have everything nice and I try very hard. I am a temperance boy. I don't drink any rum and I never will.

I learn Latin, too, when Miss Wells' class recites their lesson: *Ille, illa, illud. Sum, esse, fui.* I shall study Latin and history too. History tells about George Washington who never told a lie and Abraham Lincoln who made us free.

Perhaps I shall get on the cars some time and come to see you. Would you speak to a black boy? I shall be 8 years old next May.

George Wells

• George had been essentially adopted by Frances Wells, principal of the Trinity School in Athens, Alabama. George's letter, dated February 15, 1868, was addressed to a Sunday school class in the North.

Moses Speese and family, near Westerville, Custer County, Nebraska, 1888, photographed by Solomon D. Butcher, who characterized the family as "very highly respected citizens."

property: backlash to the Thirteenth Amendment, which abolished slavery (ratified in late 1865); the Fourteenth Amendment, which granted blacks citizenship (ratified in 1868); the Fifteenth Amendment, which granted black men the right to vote (ratified in 1870); the Civil Rights Acts of 1871 and 1875; and other progressive legislation.

Schools were torched, as happened in Memphis in 1866 when white mobs burned down twelve black schools. Children saw their teachers, black and white, beaten. Some were at home when lynch mobs came for their fathers, while others saw people dragged through the streets to be beaten, hanged, or set on fire. Some children were maimed or murdered during white rampages through black sections of towns.

Kept In (1889) by Edward Lamson Henry. This painting is one of four that the artist created based on a one-room school near Cragsmoor, New York.

Thousands in the South moved to become Northerners and Westerners because of the reign of terror: Fifty thousand people had relocated to Kansas alone by the mid-1870s. After 1877, the year President Rutherford B. Hayes pulled federal troops out of the South, widening the way for greater terrorism, more blacks prepared to migrate. Yet as the nineteenth century drew to a close, neither the North nor the West was an easy place to be. Racial discrimination was widespread from sea to shining sea.

As always, there were nonblacks who joined the black crusade for justice and equal opportunity, with around three million black girls and boys holding out hope for a brighter coming day.

The Card Trick (1880s) by John George Brown.

The McVey
children of
Boulder,
Colorado: Hazel
(standing),
Kenneth (left),
Genevieve
(right), and
Helen (seated).

PART III

Lift Every Voice and Sing

On February 12, 1900, at Stanton Institute School for Colored Children in Jacksonville, Florida, as part of the annual celebration of the birthday of Abraham Lincoln, the "Great Emancipator," some five hundred children offered up "Lift Ev'ry Voice and Sing." Out of the mouths of babes this song, written in one day by James Weldon Johnson, had its debut.

Lift ev'ry voice and sing,
Till earth and heaven ring,
Ring with the harmonies of Liberty;
Let our rejoicing rise
High as the list'ning skies,
Let it resound loud as the rolling sea.
Sing a song full of the faith that the dark past has taught us;
Sing a song full of the hope that the present has brought us;
Facing the rising sun of our new day begun,
Let us march on till victory is won.

Long after the ceremonies were concluded, the Stanton students kept singing the song, kept passing it on: to other children, to their elders, and some, in years to come, to the children they would teach. And this psalm, prayer, balm became known as the Negro National Hymn, and later, the Black National Anthem.

As Charles Johnson noted in his 1999 essay on the song's early days, "While the 'chast'ning rod' is remembered—vividly by blacks in 1900—that past is not paralyzing. Rather, those who sang these words realized they had at last 'come to the place for which [our] fathers sighed,' though the challenges and dangers they faced as a group were far from over."

Indeed, at the dawn of the twentieth century the *Plessy* v. *Ferguson* decision was four years old. This was the decision in which the United States Supreme Court gave its seal of approval to the separate-but-equal doctrine, and thus to the segregation of the races. For blacks this translated into substandard housing, lower wages, and exclusion from a host of employment, educational, and recreational opportunities. Stubborn second-classness for people of African descent would persist until the 1950s.

In the meantime and beyond, Coloreds . . . . Negroes . . . . Afro-Americans . . . . African Americans were raising up businesses, houses of worship, and civic, social, educational, and political institutions. Because so many lifted up more than their voices, across the years, against formidable odds, countless children faced the rising sun.

Women's clubs and fraternal orders, sororities and fraternities, literary societies, civil rights organizations, and other groups worked hard to lift up the children: with orphanages, food and clothing drives, private libraries, and more. There were also churches with Sunday school classes and youth auxiliaries. Paramount, of course, was schooling.

Most children attended all-black schools, with black teachers who were paid less than white teachers and who toiled, oftentimes, in shabby schoolhouses with secondhand materials—from books to blackboards. Still, many children learned—and learned well—because they wanted to learn, and because their teachers believed in them.

By dint of will and faith, a multitude of schools did their level best by their students, proving themselves worthy of grants from philanthropic organizations such as the Julius Rosenwald Fund, the Carnegie Foundation, the Phelps-Stoke Fund, and the Negro Rural School Fund (better known as the Jeanes Fund).

Among the band members in this photograph is Louis Armstrong (1901–1971). Eleven-year-old Louis (top row, shown by arrow) was sent to the Colored Waif's Home in New Orleans, Louisiana, after being arrested for firing a gun during New Year's Eve celebrations. At this reformatory, young Louis received his first formal music training, on the bugle and coronet. The future master trumpeter, known the world over as "Satchmo," was released from the reformatory when he was thirteen.

Farm Boy (1941) by Charles Alston.

Behind the scenes were the gifts of everyday people, from dollars, dimes, and nickels to chalk, fuel, land, livestock, and food. One of many examples occurred in Alabama, with the creation of the Autauga County Training School, which opened in 1921. Recalling that community's determination to qualify for a Rosenwald Fund school, M. H. Griffin, a Rosenwald building agent, wrote:

I have never seen greater human sacrifices made for the cause of education. Children without shoes on their feet gave from fifty cents to one dollar and old men and old women, whose [clothes] represented several years of wear, gave from one to five dollars. The more progressive group gave from ten to twenty-five dollars. . . . Colored men offered to pawn their cows and calves for the money and they did do just this thing.

We lived just outside the city limits. Children living beyond the city limits were supposed to go to country schools because the city schools charged the country residents $3.75 each semester for the use of books. This was a monumental sum for us because my father made from $10.00 to $14.00 a week as a combination farmer and fire tender at the brickyards. In order to get the required $3.75 each semester, my father and some of my uncles had to put their money together. It was a collective thing to raise [this] large sum of money [and] to make certain that the one child in the family attending the city school had slightly better clothing than the other children. So I had a coat that was fairly warm and a pair of shoes that was supposed to be warm but really were not. As I think about the shoes, my feet sometimes get cold even now, but I could not tell my benefactors that the shoes were not keeping me warm.

• Historian John Henrik Clarke (1915–1998), who was born in Union Springs, Alabama, and grew up in Columbus, Georgia

For the sake of schooling, many children not only parted with precious pennies, but also made long-term sacrifices: among them, walking great distances to and from school, maintaining diligence in schoolwork and chores, and foregoing playtime. Material and emotional hardships notwithstanding, a lot of children believed in themselves, believed that they could achieve.

Top: A classroom in Anthoston, Henderson County, Kentucky (1916), photographed by Lewis Hine. Bottom: This report card of Gwendolyn Bennett (1902–1981) forecasts her later shining as a writer and visual artist.

Blank V—Form 4

CENTRAL HIGH SCHOOL, HARRISBURG, PA.

Report of _Gwendolyn Bennett_ of Freshman Class for school year 1916-17

Note—The grades for scholarship are A—90, B—80-89, C—70-79, D—Condition, E—Failure.

First Term

SUBJECT	STANDING	SUBJECT	STANDING
English	a.	Phonography	
Public Speaking	a.	Typewriting	
Biology		Book-keeping	
Ancient History	a.	Spelling	
Algebra	a.	Cooking	
Latin	a.		
German		Deportment	92
French		Absent (Days)	0
Drawing	a.	Tardy (Times)	0
Business Arithmetic		Total Units to Date	

Principal.

A student who completes any course will be graduated regardless of required units. In case a student does not complete a course he may graduate if he has completed 16 units, 9 of which are required. The required units are: 3 of English, 2 of Foreign Language, 2 of Mathematics, 1 of History, and 1 of Science.

Parents will co-operate by making home conditions for study as favorable as possible. Absence and lateness materially affect the progress of the best students, hence great effort and sacrifice should be made to avoid both in every possible case.

Clumped in the vastness of the prairie, [Fort Scott, Kansas,] was proud of its posture as part of a free state, while clinging grimly to the ways of the Deep South. . . . The grade school was segregated but the high school wasn't—mainly because the town fathers couldn't scrounge up enough money to build a separate one. But even inside those walls of meager learning, black students had to accommodate themselves to the taste of salt. We were not allowed to participate in sports or attend social functions. The class advisers warned us against seeking higher education, adding, "You were meant to be maids and porters." College for us, they said, would be a waste of time and money.

• Photographer, painter, writer, and filmmaker Gordon Parks (b. 1912)

For many, reaching their potential included being well-mannered and all else that reflected good "hometraining." Civic duty and neighborliness were part and parcel of personal growth and development. In recalling their childhood in Raleigh, North Carolina, the sisters Sadie and Bessie Delany (1889–1999 and 1891–1995 respectively) remembered that while their father occasionally shopped at the local A & P (he had a "weakness" for its Eight O'Clock coffee), he went out of his way to purchase most of the family's groceries from a black merchant. "So Papa would drag us all the way to Mr. Jones's store to buy groceries, since Mr. Jones was a Negro. It not only was inconvenient to shop at Mr. Jones's, it was more expensive. We used to complain about it, because we passed the A & P on the way. We would say, 'Papa, why can't we just shop at the A & P?' And Papa would say, 'Mr. Jones needs our money to live on, and the A & P does not. We are buying our economic freedom.'"

A teacher and her pupils outside a school in Athens, Georgia in the early twentieth century.

Success in life was not to be measured in terms of money and personal advancement, but rather the goal must be the richest and highest development of one's own potential.

A love for learning, a ceaseless quest for truth in all its fullness—this my father taught. . . . [H]e firmly believed that the heights of knowledge must be scaled by the freedom-seeker. Latin, Greek, philosophy, history, literature—all the treasures of learning must be the Negro's heritage as well.

So for me in high school there would be four years of Latin and then in college four more years of Latin and Greek. Closely my father watched my studies, and was with me page by page through Virgil and Homer and the other classics in which he was well grounded. He was my first teacher in public speaking, and long before my days as a class orator and college debater there were the evenings of recitations at home, where his love for the eloquent and meaningful word and his insistence on purity of diction made their impress.

• Actor, singer, and activist Paul Robeson (1898–1976), whose father escaped slavery as a young man

A youth brigade of a YMCA city clean-up campaign in Chicago, Illinois, in 1919.

The Black Church played a tremendous role in seeding and cultivating high ideals in the young, along with a range of skills. The church was so much more than a place of worship. Whether Baptist, Congregational, Lutheran, Pentecostal, Presbyterian, African Methodist Episcopal, or another denomination, by and large, the church was a black community's hub—school, day care center, community center, clothing bank, food pantry, concert hall, town hall. It was where many boys and girls received their first training in the arts (the choirs, the bands, the seasonal pageants), in public speaking (Children's Day

Widower Reverend John Brooks with his children (c. 1907).

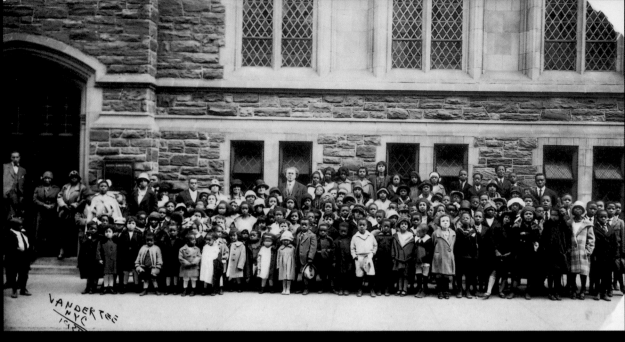

Reverend Adam Clayton Powell Sr. with his Sunday School class at Abyssinian Baptist Church in Harlem, New York, photographed by James VanDerZee in 1925.

I was interested in drawing and sketching. My [twin brother Morgan] also. The earliest was copying from pictures in magazines, and from that we went into charcoal and pastels and then into oil painting. My brother and I read an article about soap sculpture from bars of Ivory soap. The large bath size. So we both got involved in making figures out of cakes of Ivory soap. The principal at Dunbar High was impressed, so he put them on display in the lobby at school . . . which was uplifting, which encouraged us.

• Marvin Smith (b. 1910). The future photographers Marvin and Morgan Smith (d. 1993) were born in Nicholsville, Kentucky, and raised in Lexington.

I remember the annual ritual of filling Christmas stockings for children in an orphanage, and the many days when I came home from school to find [my mother] packing a tray with a hot dinner for an ailing neighbor. The neighbor might be a close friend or just a "speaking" acquaintance. . . .

On our block, early morning sweeping of porches and sidewalks was a daily ritual. With my little broom, I would join [my father]. When we had finished, we would walk the length of the block, greeting each neighbor. On these walks he would teach me to see the things in nature which fascinated him, and by carefully removing any obstacle on the sidewalk lest "someone stumble over it," he taught me about thoughtfulness as well.

• Artist, teacher, and children's book author Margery Wheeler Brown, who grew up in Atlanta, Georgia, on Johnson Avenue, one of the city's enclaves of middle-class blacks

programs and other events), in leadership skills (the youth auxiliaries), and in being "a credit to the race."

Amid the training at church, school, and home that children received, there was all manner of fun to be had as well—trading cards, shooting aggies, playing made-up games, rounds of hide-and-seek, or a bit of kick-the-can. Some had the treat of seeing baseball games between various Negro League teams that began to flourish in the 1920s. A highlight for others was sitting ringside—by radio—and cheering for Joe Louis, "The Brown Bomber."

Doodlebug (1992) by Bessie Nickens, from Walking the Log: Memories of a Southern Childhood (1994).

A doodlebug is just a little bug. In sandy areas, you put your head close to the sand and you said, "Doodlebug, doodlebug, yer house on fire!" And a little bug appeared, a doodlebug. We kids, my brothers and sisters and neighbors, a bunch of us would get together and go out and just call them up. We never did touch them. . . .

And of course we all used to fly kites. My brother made kites. . . . All the neighborhood kids made kites. They were made out of news-paper. You'd get some sticks and cross them up, and stick the paper on there. Sometimes my brother and I would fly a kite together.

• Bessie Nickens (b. 1906), born in Sligo, Louisiana, spent her childhood in various towns in Louisiana and Texas

Christmas Morning, Breakfast (1945) by Horace Pippin, born in West Chester, Pennsylvania, and raised in Goshen, New York. The absence of a father in the painting suggests that this painting is autobiographical: When Horace was about ten, his father died.

Well, Billikens, how did you enjoy Christmas and New Years? My, but I had a fine time. How do you like the snow? . . .

The merry cries of the children rang in my ears, and, Oh, how I had to laugh when I saw a boy knock the hat off of a big fat man. Then the man turned around, and, Oh, how that boy ran home. Bob had his dog hitched to his sled and several of the larger boys were making a sled. Pete was washing William's face in the snow for hitting Evelyn, his girl, with a snow ball. . . . —BUD

• From a 1923 edition of the *Defender Junior*, brainchild of the *Chicago Defender*. "Bud" was the pseudonym used by the section's editor, at this time Willard Motley (1912–1965) who grew up to be a novelist. The offerings of the *Defender Junior* included jokes, recipes, stories, poetry, as well as photos and letters of members of the Billiken Club.

Some children even became famous—such as the Philadelphians Fayard and Harold Nicholas, sons of vaudeville musicians, who performed dazzling tap dance acts as "The Nicholas Kids." Their great break came in 1931 with an appearance on the radio show, the *Horn and Hardart Kiddie Hour*. "That was the first time we danced on the radio," Fayard remembered. "We couldn't do any splits because no one could see that. But they could hear those taps."

Not all child stars received rave reviews from their people, especially not those who made a career playing the "pickaninny." "Generally, [the pickaninny] was a . . . little screwball creation whose eyes popped, whose hair stood on end with the least excitement," explains film historian Donald Bogle. He credits Thomas Edison as "a pioneer in the exploitation and exploration of this type when he presented *Ten Pickaninnies* in 1904, a forerunner of the Hal Roach *Our Gang* series."

Sunshine Sammy became one of the highest-paid child actors in the 1920s for his "pickaninny" portrayals. There was also Allen Clayton Hoskins—"Farina"—who appeared in more than one hundred *Our Gang* movie shorts, the last in 1930. This was the year that five-year-old Matt Beard Jr. made his debut as derby-donning "Stymie." Next came Billie "Buckwheat" Thomas.

GEORGE THATCHER'S GREATEST MINSTRELS

"HELLO! MY BABY."

Opposite page, left: Fayard (b. 1917) and Harold (1921–2000) Nicholas, in the 1930s. This dancing duo became stars of stage, screen, and cabaret as The Nicholas Brothers. Opposite page, right: Philippa Duke Schuyler (1931–1967) was composing for piano at four and playing Mozart at five. At the 1940 World's Fair, New York City's mayor Fiorello LaGuardia declared June 19, 1940, Philippa Duke Schuyler Day. Left: Derogatory images of black men, women, and children, as in this 1899 poster, were common in the early twentieth century.

We were among the first blacks to vacation on Martha's Vineyard. It is not unlikely that the Island, in particular Oak Bluffs, had a larger number of vacationing blacks than any other section of the country. . . .

Every day, the young mothers took their children to a lovely stretch of beach and scattered along it in little pools. . . .

Sometimes the children took their shovels and pails and built castles together. It was a pretty scene. The blacks in all their beautiful colors, pink and gold and brown and ebony. The whites in summer's bronze.

The days were full. There were berries to pick, a morning's adventure. There were band concerts for an evening's stroll. There were invitations to lemonade and cookies and whist.

• Essayist, novelist, and short story writer Dorothy West (1907–1998)

A young boy totes a bucket of coal in this photograph taken sometime during the early twentieth century in either Washington, D.C., or New York City.

There were children who, perhaps, would have gladly acted the fool if doing so would have rescued them from the poverty in which they lived. Poverty meant children selling pecans along a road in Georgia, chopping sugarcane in Louisiana, chopping and picking cotton in Mississippi, working the orchards in California, or being domestic workers in New York, Massachusetts, South Carolina, Virginia, and elsewhere.

Where poverty was abysmal, children might have slept on the floor or in a bed with five or more others. They may have had no change of clothes, or money for a doctor, or enough to eat. Many had a slim chance of living to be "grownfolks." In 1940, for example, black babies were almost twice as likely as white babies to die before reaching their first birthday.

They'd start you watching young ones and getting water from the spring. That's on the day you stood up! By four, you'd be doing feeding and a little field work, and you'd always be minding somebody. By six, you'd be doing small pieces in a tub every wash day and you'd bring all the clear water for rinsing the clothes. By eight, you'd be able to mind children, do cooking, and wash. If you wasn't trained full by ten—you was thought to be slow. Still, even if you was slow, you had to do!

By ten you'd be trained—our people was seeing to that. You was thought to be 'bout grown as far as your training. Especially a girl. Your training was early and hard. No girl I know wasn't training for work out by ten. . . . Girls are started early with work—no play ever for a girl. . . . Work, work, work. No play, 'cause they told you, "Life was to be hardest on you—always."

• Pernella Ross, who grew up in North Carolina

Commonly referred to as *Girl at Gee's Bend, Alabama,* this photograph of ten-year-old Artelia Bendolph was taken in April 1927 by Arthur Rothstein.

Still, out of poverty came many lights—writer Richard Wright; photographer, writer, and filmmaker Gordon Parks; trumpet king Louis Armstrong; and dancer, singer, and actress Eartha Kitt, among others.

During the first three decades of the twentieth century, many black people sought to improve their lot by relocating. This was the Great Migration, when an estimated two million men, women, and children left the South because of the boll weevil that had destroyed the cotton crop, terrorist groups such as the Ku Klux Klan, and a range of inequalities from schooling to housing and employment.

They went to the big cities—New York, Chicago, Detroit, St. Louis. Some children found better schools and their parents, better jobs. Others found that their move resulted in hardly any change at all: They became another bleak face in a different crowd of poor.

Panel #58 of Jacob Lawrence's sixty-panel series *The Migration of the Negro* (1941). The original caption to this panel is: "In the North the Negro had better educational facilities."

A family from the rural south that has just arrived in Chicago (c. 1919).

The move could be a mixed blessing for the children whose parents went West or North without them. Sometimes parents were able to send money, clothing, and toys back home; yet this meant that many girls and boys went missing their parents for a while. Sometimes the missing stretched on for years, because parents were unable to get established enough to send for their children. Sometimes it was the children who migrated to take jobs as domestics or in mills, mines, and factories; sometimes it was the children who sent money back home.

When the Klan Passes By (c. 1940) by James A. Porter.

Violence, and fear of violence, was another hardship many young people faced, from abusive employers and even parents, as well as peers who led a life of crime. Added to these was the violence born of race hatred. In the thousands of lynchings of blacks and the scores of white riots in black communities between 1900 and 1940, there were young lives damaged or destroyed. Many who were not physically harmed grew up with memories of horrible hostilities. The poor got the worst of it, but children of the prosperous knew fear and humiliations as well.

Ticket stub for a segregated theater.

The native of Jacksonville, Florida, anthropologist and former president of Spelman College Johnnetta Betsch Cole (b. 1936) recalled that while her family's status provided some "buffers," there was no "refuge from racism." (Her maternal grandfather cofounded Afro-American Life Insurance Company and the black resort American Beach on Amelia Island). Johnnetta would never forget being assaulted at the age of three with that soul-crushing word "nigger." Many a summer's day she looked longingly at the for-whites-only swimming pool in a park across the street from her elegant home at 1748 Jefferson Street. She also vividly remembered "traveling North with my parents and, as we moved through the Southern states at night, being terrified that the car would break down and the Ku Klux Klan would come."

When I went to school, I read the history books that glorify the white race and describe the Negro either as a clown and a fool or a beast capable of very hard work in excessive heat. I discovered the background of chattel slavery behind this madness of race prejudice. . . . But when I went home to the good books and the wonderful music and the gentle, intelligent parents, I could see no reason for prejudice on the basis of a previous condition of servitude. . . .

Then I began to daydream. . . . Someday, just as chattel slavery ended, this injustice will also end; this internal suffering will cease; this ache inside for understanding will exist no longer. Someday, I said, when I am fully grown, I will understand, and be able to do something about it. I will write books that will prove the history texts were distorted. I will write books about colored people who have colored faces, books that will not make me ashamed when I read them.

- Margaret Walker (1915–1998), who was born in Birmingham, Alabama, and whose best-known works are the poem "For My People" and the novel *Jubilee*

The Brownies' Book, a monthly magazine for "the Children of the Sun," premiered in January 1920.

"Doesn't Dolly Look Like Me?" was the original caption to this photo.

Black children were also mistreated in children's literature. Rarely were they portrayed positively by white writers and illustrators. Helen Bannerman's *The Story of Little Black Sambo* was hardly the only offending book. *Watermelon Pete and Other Stories* was among other such books created for the entertainment and edification of white children.

Many parents were, therefore, grateful to Effie Lee Newsome, Jessie Fauset, Langston Hughes, and other writers who produced uplifting prose and poetry. *Negro Art, Music and Rhyme* by Helen Adele Whiting and *The Child's Story of the Negro* by Jane D. Shackelford (both illustrated by Lois Mailou Jones) are two examples. These books were published in 1938 by Associated Publishers, founded by the "Father of Black History," Carter G. Woodson. It was Woodson who, in 1926, launched the forerunner of Black History Month, Negro History Week, which offered heritage activities for children as well as adults. Among the many books that Woodson not only published but also wrote were several for the young (among them *African Heroes and Heroines*).

While so many in black America labored to nurture and nourish the young, there was an undermining, from within, of their self-esteem. One of the legacies of centuries of degradation was a distorted concept of beauty. It was therefore commonplace for adults to adore the

Nancy Douglas Bowlin (c. 1937) dressed for her first holy communion at St. Thomas the Apostle Roman Catholic Church in Harlem, New York.

light-skinned child. The straighter the hair, the better.

Many adults thought they were doing good and right by children with the straightening comb, lye, ineffective and sometimes harmful bleaching creams, clothespins on noses, and warnings to stay out of the sun—but wounds ran deep. "I remember that as a young boy I used to look in the mirror and I would curse my color, my blackness," recollected Leon Walter Tillage, born in the 1930s in a town outside Raleigh, North Carolina.

Light-skinned, long-haired children were affected, too. Some grew up with the delusion that they were superior. Some suffered taunts and boot kicks from their peers who resented the preferential treatment they received or envied them their color, or their hair, or both.

Many children did not have such problems. Frequently this was because they had parents who cherished the African in them: people like the parents of Nancy Douglas Bowlin, (b. 1927). "I knew as a child that my father's ancestors were Yoruba, and my father especially impressed upon me how important it was for me to know my roots, and to be proud of my African heritage." In her seventies Bowlin could still hear her father's words: "Remember who you are." She also recalled that although she never flatly protested her hair being straightened—"it was the thing to do"— she never felt that straightened hair became her.

As America moved toward mid-century, young

Gamin (1930) by Augusta Savage, who used her young nephew Ellis Ford as the model.

Top: *Negro Boys on Easter Morning on the South Side of Chicago* (April 1941) by Russell Lee. Bottom: Author Langston Hughes, with young fans, in Atlanta, Georgia, in 1947, during a Negro History Week event.

blacks were, of course, concerned with issues bigger than skin color and hair texture. The work of the National Association for the Advancement of Colored People (NAACP) and other organizations raised the consciousness of children as well as adults. The young were as eager for equal opportunities as their elders. They wanted justice and the freedom to be somebody in the larger society.

With World War II came new vigor in the civil rights crusade. Black valor in the armed services, displayed most famously by the Tuskegee Airmen, fueled many children with pride and the courage to stand up for themselves.

Jim McWilliams, of Fairfield, Alabama, was one such braveheart. In 1944, twelve-year-old Jim led a group of *Birmingham News* delivery boys on a strike. "Each day the black newsboys—but not the white—would have to unload the news delivery trucks and carry heavy bundles of one hundred papers into the delivery office. Mr. Morris, the white station manager, parceled papers out to all the newsboys, and we'd leave for our segregated neighborhoods. One day when I arrived and saw the papers stacked in the street and the white newsboys waiting inside, I got angry. I told my buddies it was unfair for us to carry the papers inside and they agreed."

The newsboys stood firm, and after the second week of the strike their demand for fair treatment was met. "From then on all the newsboys carried papers in from the street. So he wouldn't have to deal with us black newsboys, Mr. Morris put me in charge of parceling out our papers, collecting our receipts, and he paid me extra for the work."

If black youth were to have equal opportunity, the end of segregated schooling was critical, many believed. As the architect of the NAACP Legal and Educational Defense Fund, Charles Hamilton Houston, put it:

> *These apparent senseless discriminations in education against Negroes have a very definite objective on the part of the ruling whites to curb the young and prepare them to accept an inferior position in American life without protest or struggle.*

Following several successful lawsuits against colleges and universities that had refused to admit blacks, the NAACP went to work on behalf of schoolchildren.

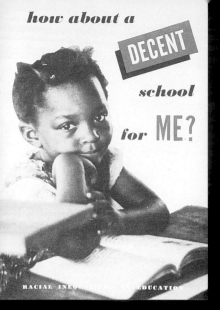

how about a DECENT *school for* ME?

RACIAL INEQUALITY IN EDUCATION

The linchpin was the case that brought Linda Carol Brown of Topeka, Kansas, into the spotlight.

Nine-year-old Linda Brown had been prohibited from attending Sumner School, a public school near her home. Instead, like many other black children in her neighborhood, Linda's journey to school included walking through a railroad switching yard, crossing a big, heavily trafficked street and waiting—sometimes for an hour, sometimes in nasty weather—for the bus that would take her to a school about two miles away. All this because Sumner, a few blocks away from Linda's home, was for white children only.

Linda's father, Oliver Brown, went to the NAACP's local branch for help, and joined with about a dozen other parents in a lawsuit against the Topeka school board for the integration of Sumner. The case, heard in the summer of 1951, was eventually bundled with several similar cases in the South and known collectively as *Brown* v. *Board of Education*. The NAACP's chief counsel, Thurgood Marshall, was serving as the lead lawyer by the time the case reached the U.S. Supreme Court.

The decision was handed down on May 17, 1954, with the Court delivering a unanimous decision that overturned the earlier ruling in *Plessy* v. *Ferguson*. "We conclude," said the justices, "that in the field of education the doctrine of 'separate but equal' has no place. Separate educational facilities are inherently unequal."

Some black children rejoiced over the Brown decision; others were wary. In either case, children who had only attended all-black schools did not really know what it would mean to go to school with white children. Better facilities? Better materials? At what price?

Opposite page, top: The cover of a 1946 NAACP pamphlet. Opposite page, bottom: *Boy with Tire* (1952) by Hughie Lee-Smith captures the mix of yearning and forlornness many young people felt. Above: Twelve-year-old Cassius Clay in 1954. At age fourteen this native of Louisville, Kentucky, won his first Golden Glove. At age eighteen, at the 1960 Olympics in Rome, he won a gold medal. Four years later he changed his name to Muhammad Ali.

At 2:30 P.M. on the afternoon of May 17, 1954, I was sitting in Mr. Bland's eighth-grade science class at the battered desk on the outside row near a bank of open windows.... The school was Benjamin A. Graves Junior High, an imposing old colonnaded redbrick building [in Richmond, Virginia]....

"—has just been handed down and it will change all of our lives." Mr. Bland was talking. I wasn't listening but everyone else appeared to be, which was unusual.

"What did he say?" I asked the girl in front of me. Mr. Bland heard.

"I said, Randall, that the United States Supreme Court has outlawed public school segregation. The schools will be integrated."

I was stunned. The class was quiet, reactions difficult to read. If this warranted a celebration, it got none from Mr. Bland's science class....

I did not want to go to school with white people.... I wanted the right to go anywhere I wished to go. I also wanted the right not to go.... I'll concede that I was more than a little frightened. After all, white people had spent the better part of four hundred years conspiring to convince me of my innate intellectual inferiority. They had made some headway. And I hated them for that. At thirteen, I only sometimes thought I was smart. I secretly believed I was special.... But the doubts about competitive ability had been well sown. Also by age thirteen, I had intuitively developed the cardinal guidepost for emotional health: the Never Wannabe Rule. Never want to be with people who don't want to be with you....

The bell was about to ring....

My mind wandered. I was thinking about how white students might be accepting the news at Hermitage, Highland Springs, and Thomas Jefferson. I couldn't visualize these schools. I'd never seen them. But I pictured white faces, some tear-streaked, some angry.

Don't flatter yourselves. I'm not coming to your school.

• Randall Robinson (b. 1941), founder of TransAfrica, a lobbying group that focuses on U.S. policy as it relates to Africa, the Caribbean, and Latin America

During this time of great expectations for some and deep dread for others, one of the most publicized murders of a young person occurred: that of a fourteen-year-old from Chicago, Emmett Till. In the summer of 1955, when Emmett was visiting family in Money, Mississippi, two white men went after him because they had been told that he had been disrespectful to a white woman in a store. These men, Roy Bryant and J. W. Milam—the woman's husband and his brother-in-law—yanked Emmett from his uncle's home, brutally beat him, shot him in the head, and, after wrapping a gin-mill fan around his neck with barbed wire, dumped his body in the Tallahatchie River.

As the search for the body went on, my older sister [Dorrie] and I . . . wanted to be the first in line to buy the *Hattiesburg American*. Each day we poured over the clippings of the lynching we kept in our scrapbook, and cried: Emmett Till was about our age. . . . When we saw his bloated body in *Jet* magazine, we asked each other "How could they do that to him? He's only a young boy."

• Sociologist and one-time president of Howard University Joyce Ladner (b. 1943), who grew up in Hattiesburg, Mississippi. In reaction to what had happened to Emmett Till, along with her sister, young Joyce got involved in the NAACP chapter in Jacksonville, Mississippi, headed by Medgar Evers.

News of this murder was international. The horror was impressed on the minds of millions because Emmett's mother insisted on an open casket funeral. She wanted the world to see what had been done to her child. Thanks to photographers, the world did see, and many would never forget. That Emmett's murderers were found not guilty by an all-white, all-male jury increased the outrage and encouraged others to campaign for social justice.

During this era, many young people stood up to be counted. One was Claudette Colvin of Birmingham, Alabama. In March 1955, nine months before Rosa Parks carried out her famous act of defiance in Montgomery, fifteen-year-old Claudette was arrested for refusing to give up her bus seat to a white passenger, as the law required of blacks.

Many other young people contributed to the movement by agreeing to be in the vanguard of school integration. In some communities they began attending heretofore all-white schools without incident. In many instances, however, the new black students were not so fortunate. Along with physical harm for some came emotional trauma for others.

In 1957, while most teenage girls were listening to Buddy Holly's "Peggy Sue," watching Elvis gyrate, and collecting crinoline slips, I was escaping the hanging rope of a lynch mob, dodging lighted sticks of dynamite, and washing away burning acid sprayed into my eyes.

During my junior year in high school, I lived at the center of a violent civil rights conflict. In 1954, the Supreme Court had decreed an end to segregated schools. Arkansas Governor Orval Faubus and states' rights segregationists defied that ruling. President Eisenhower was compelled to confront Faubus—to use U.S. soldiers to force him to obey the law of the land. . . . At the center of the controversy were nine black children who wanted only to have the opportunity for a better education.

On our first day at Central High, Governor Faubus dispatched gun-toting Arkansas National Guard soldiers to prevent us from entering. Mother and I got separated from the others. The two of us narrowly escaped a rope-carrying lynch mob of men and women shouting that they'd kill us rather than see me go to school with their children.

- Melba Pattillo Beals (b. 1942), one of the "Little Rock Nine," as the students who integrated Central High are known. Melba's fellow "warriors" were Minnijean Brown (Trickey), Elizabeth Eckford, Ernest Green, Thelma Mothershed (Wair), Gloria Ray (Karlmark), Terrence Roberts, Jefferson Thomas, and Carlotta Walls (LaNier).

Opposite page: September 26, 1957, at Central High in Little Rock, Arkansas, photographed by Arnold Sachs.

The Problem We All Live With (1964) by Norman Rockwell. This painting was a tribute to Ruby Bridges, who in 1960, at age six, became the first black student at William Frantz Elementary School in New Orleans, Louisiana. Whites protested by pulling their children out of the school. For months Ruby Bridges was the only student who attended that school.

Young blacks heard about white parents who removed their children from school, preferring to let their children go untaught rather than to learn alongside black students. Blacks were aware that in some communities, whites abandoned the public schools, sending their children instead to private academies, which greatly increased in the wake of the Brown decision. Some public schools defied the order by failing to open for the school year, as happened in Birmingham, Alabama, in September 1963.

On the fifteenth day of that month, two weeks after the historic March on Washington for Jobs and Freedom led by Martin Luther King Jr., four Birmingham children became martyrs for the cause of racial justice: Addie Mae Collins (age fourteen), Denise McNair (age eleven), Carole Robertson (age fourteen), and

Cynthia Wesley (age fourteen). These girls, were in Sunday school when a bomb went off in Sixteenth Street Baptist Church—a bomb planted by members of the Ku Klux Klan, a bomb that not only killed these four little girls but also injured many, including twenty other children.

For every child maimed or murdered by racists, there were ten, twenty, hundreds who were emotionally scarred by the news of what happened to many civil

From the "Children's Crusade" in Birmingham, Alabama, in spring 1963, photographed by Bob Adelman. After many adults (including Reverend Martin Luther King Jr.) had been arrested for peaceful demonstrations, a host of children joined the crusade. On May 3, more than a thousand young people, trained in nonviolence, marched out of Sixteenth Street Baptist Church to downtown Birmingham, where the police hauled them off to jail. The next day hundreds more youngsters joined the campaign, flooding the streets and stores (many braving police dogs and water cannons). All the young crusaders helped bring the city to a standstill: immobilizing the police, tying up traffic, and thus forcing the power structure to start negotiations on civil rights concerns.

On a May day in Los Angeles, in 1970, when I was eleven years old, two things happened that changed my life.

I had taken to riding the RTD bus down to the Black Panthers' small store-front office on Broadway. The walls of the reception area were covered with posters of Huey Newton sitting in a wicker chair...a rifle, and "Free Huey" flyers were stacked all around the office. Behind the desk a huge flag hung on the wall with a black panther on it that looked like it was ready to leap.

For a few hours after school each day, I ran errands, passed out flyers, and listened to a beautiful sister with a big Afro rap about some guy named Mao. ...Afterward, they would let the kids who'd helped out that day eat all the cookies and doughnuts we wanted.

On the day that Huey Newton was to be released from prison, I took a stand of my own at West Athens Elementary School. ...I refused to stay in the classroom while [Mrs. Paget] read *Little Black Sambo* aloud to the class. There was something about that story that made me angry, something in the way Mrs. Paget read it that gave me the distinct feeling that Sambo was in the classroom and she fully expected him to come forward holding a big plate of flapjacks.

"Don't be a nigger, Ross," she said as I walked out of the classroom.

It was my first real experience with the issue of race, and her words made me conscious of my blackness in a way that all of the black power and black pride slogans at the Panther office had not.

• Anthony Ross. The second life-changing event of that day occurred when a white boy insulted young Anthony—"His voice carried that same tone I'd heard in Mrs. Paget's voice." In anger, Anthony "socked" the kid, and made him hand over whatever money he had (a few dollars). For this Anthony ended up in jail, where he was beaten up by police officers —"They started hitting and kicking my whole body." He was released after spending a few hours in a cell.

ights crusaders. These horrors include the assassinations of Medgar Evers and Martin Luther King Jr.; the beatings of Freedom Riders; the billy clubs, water cannons, and dogs that police officers unleashed on thousands of peaceful demonstrators.

Young blacks saw that their presence in many formerly all-white schools was resisted year after year—and not only in the South. In the late 1960s there were ugly incidents revolving around school integration in Boston, Massachusetts, Denver, Colorado, and elsewhere in the North and West. In 1968, for instance, in the Bensonhurst section of Brooklyn, New York, Tracy Price Thompson, who was "soooo excited" about her first day of elementary school, had no ordinary walk up the front steps of her school. At the top of the steps a crowd of men and women chanted, "Two, four, six, eight . . . we don't wanna in-te-grate." They carried signs that read KEEP OUR SCHOOLS PURE and NO NIGGERS ALLOWED.

It is true that the Civil Rights movement had a huge impact on the lives of millions of black youth (whether they knew it or not), but not all young people were heavily influenced by this Christian-based movement, with its integrationist thrust. Some black children were members of secular and religious organizations that believed racial separatism to be a good thing. There were also those who were simply more attracted to Black Power activists who were in favor of desegregation but looked askance at integration. These included the Black Panthers, who operated breakfast programs and other projects for children in distressed areas of cities such as Chicago, Detroit, Los Angeles, Newark, and New York City.

One impact of the Black Power movement was a greater interest in and information about African heritage. Thus, the rise in children (along with adults) wearing their natural hair in Afros and braids, and donning African clothing such as the dashiki. Also increasingly on school

A Black Power button, featuring two icons of the movement. "R[ ]On!" was an affirmation and show of support, akin to "Amen!" [   ]ven "You go, girl!" The clench[ ] fist symbolized unity and strength.

All around us the landmarks of our childhood—Eddie's corner store, the Big Dipper supermarket, and the storage company across the street from our elementary school—were looted or in flames. . . .

Some of those arrested, like my brother, were teenagers. Others were out-of-work factory employees, family men angered over what they believed was society's failure to open the doors of opportunity to black men and women.

I was too young, at age eleven, to understand all these feelings. . . .

On that day, the third of what ultimately would be eight days of the Detroit riot, I was not among the group of looters and rioters. I was only a fascinated observer.

That would change. . . .

I ran to the front door, opened it, cracked the screen door, and peered outside. I saw five, maybe six, National Guardsmen milling around the sidewalk. . . . They looked like aliens, like people from a foreign land, with riot masks covering their faces, bulky suits covering their bodies, and rifles in hand.

I opened the door wider.

"Shut that door, Ron!" yelled my mother, who rarely, if ever shouted.

I stared at the Guardsmen, who suddenly turned and looked. At me. They charged. Startled by the urgency of their onrush, I paused, darted inside, and slammed the door.

I felt something that I'd never felt before—bone-chilling fear. . . . I couldn't gather myself. I couldn't cry out. . . .

[A]nd then I heard my mother, her voice both a plea and demand, shout: "Please, please don't hurt my baby," and I felt her slight body engulf me. I felt her heartbeat against mine, and felt her tears fall onto my face.

I looked up at the screen door. The men wearing the masks and carrying the rifles were gone.

• Ronald K. Fitten, who grew up to be a journalist

rosters around the nation appeared names such as *Kwame* (born on Saturday), *Aisha* (life), *Jamila* (beautiful), and *Malik* (master). This was all part of parents' efforts to ground their children in black identity and foster pride in them. For this reason many parents embraced Kwanzaa, the weeklong heritage celebration (December 26–January 1), which began in the mid-1960s.

In the midst and in the wake of the tumultuous 1960s and 1970s, with that era's many movements (civil rights, black power, feminist, and antiwar), most young blacks were more focused on typical youth preoccupations than anything else. There were varieties of play: hula hoop and hopscotch, skating and all manner of ball games, skully, jacks and pick-up-sticks, freeze tag, ring-a-levio, double Dutch, and hot-peas-and-butter, which is very similar to the game of hide-the-switch played

Double Dutch Series: Do It Anyway You Wanna (1985) by Tina Dunkley.

in the nineteenth century. Too, there was puppy love. There were proms and after-church big family dinners; trips to zoos, museums, the movies, and amusement parks. There was keeping up with Morrie Turner's "Wee Pals" and other comic strips.

Rowland J. Martin Jr. (c. 1961) at the annual rodeo and carnival at Joe Freeman Coliseum in San Antonio, Texas. It was open to everyone, unlike some local amusement parks that set aside days for "negroes" and "colored people" only.

Before rap music came out of the South Bronx, one could hear Puerto Ricans and African Americans playing their drums in the summertime. The year before I went off to college, I knew my inability to dance saved me from running with the wrong crowd. My parents kept my brother, sister, and me off the streets. Only when we were older did we realize that we had avoided jail, pregnancy, death, and the scars that come with early adulthood. If my brother was saved by candles, holy water, and religion, then it was the "glove" that allowed me to survive the housing projects and killing fields.

I was very good at playing baseball. My signature move was leaping against a fence, sticking my glove out over it, and taking away homers. I liked to hang on the fence, giving the hitter the impression I had missed the baseball. As soon as I spotted the home run trot, the swagger, the clapping of the hands, the boast or yell, then like a magician I would stick my glove up showing the ball to all.

• Poet E. Ethelbert Miller (b. 1950), director of the African American Resource Center at Howard University

Youngsters were also into a range of hobbies. In the early 1960s young Chuck, of Evanston, Illinois, was a ravenous reader, especially crazy

for comic books—spending about a dollar a week on ten- and twelve-cent DC and Marvel comic books. They inspired his dream to be a cartoonist. "From the Evanston Public Library I lugged home every book on drawing, cartooning, and collections of early comic art . . . and pored over them." Chuck poured most of his money into art supplies: allowance money and money earned from his paper route and after-school jobs. In 1966, at age seventeen, he made his debut as a professional cartoonist, and went on to produce a huge body of comic art. Along the way, he made a greater mark as a writer, known professionally as Charles Johnson, whose numerous awards include a 1998 MacArthur Foundation "Genius" Award.

Top: Brumsic Brandon Jr.'s comic strip "Luther" (1968–1986) was named in honor of Martin Luther King, Jr. Luther and his buddies, including Pee Wee, Hardcore, and Oreo, also appeared in six books, among them *Luther Raps*. Bottom, left: Charles Johnson's full-page cartoon for his high school newspaper, *The Evanstonian* (June 3, 1966). Just above the lower left corner, Johnson and his classmate Tom Reitze are being whisked away by Wonder Wildkit, the cartoon superhero the two boys co-created. Bottom, right: A self-portrait of seventeen-year-old Charles Johnson.

Around the time that young Chuck was living his dream as a cartoonist in Illinois, in the Bronx, New York, fourteen-year-old Neil de Grasse Tyson (b. 1958) was walking people's dogs and saving up his earnings for the telescope he so desired—a giant step toward his eventual career: astrophysicist.

While young Neil was training his sights on the stars, in Flint, Michigan twins Paula and Pamela McGee (b. 1962) were spending heaps of time at age nine shooting hoops in their backyard. Their passion for basketball would lead them to become hardwood stars in high school and at the University of Southern California (USC). In the 1980s the twins led USC's Lady Trojans to back-to-back NCAA championships. (Pam was also a member of the 1984 U.S. women's basketball team, both women went on to play professionally overseas, and in the 1990s Pam played for a time in the WNBA, with Paula as her agent.)

Left to right: Paula and Pamela McGee at age fifteen.

Television, a staple in American homes by the late 1960s, provided another source of fun for black children, as it did for other children. As the overwhelming majority of people on television (commercials included) were white, especially thrilling for black youth were appearances of blacks on the screen. Prime times were when the Supremes, the Temptations, and other performers appeared on programs such as *Hullabaloo*, *American Bandstand*, and the *Ed Sullivan Show*. When Don Cornelius's black-oriented dance show, *Soul Train*, came along in 1970—wow!

The Jackson 5 at the London Palladium in October 1972 (foreground: Michael; left to right: Tito, Marlon, Jackie, Jermaine). This group of brothers from Gary, Indiana—heartthrobs all—was a Motown super-success, one of the hottest groups—internationally—of the 1960s and 1970s (there was even a Jackson 5 cartoon!).

From 1968 to 1971 many youngsters tuned in to *Julia*, far less interested in the series's title character played by Diahann Carroll than in her adorable son, Corey (Marc Copage). Similarly, when it came to the first black family sitcom, *Good Times* (1974–1979), young people's favorite characters were the mini-militant Michael (Ralph Carter) and his older brother, the artist in the family, J.J. (Jimmy Walker), with his trademark line "Dyn-O-Mite!"

Other television draws of the 1970s and beyond included the cartoon cutups of *Fat Albert and the Cosby Kids* (1972–1979) (and later *The New Fat Albert Show*, 1979–1984) and the sitcom *What's Happening!!* (1976–1979), which turned on the antics of aspiring writer Raj (Ernest Thomas) and his sidekicks Dwayne with the "Hey, Hey, Hey!" (Haywood Nelson Jr.) and the locker-dancing Rerun (Fred

Berry), with frequent wit and sass from Raj's little sister, Dee (Danielle Spencer). There was also *The Cosby Show* (1984–1992), which featured a type of black family—and thus a type of black youth—rarely spotted on television or in film: upper middle class. Very popular as well were *The Cosby Show* spin-off, *A Different World* (1987–1993); *The Fresh Prince of Bel Air* (1990–1996); and *Family Matters* (1989–1998), where an initially minor character played by Jaleel White became the sitcom's main attraction: the nerdy, needy, needling Steve Urkel. Although some of these shows had their critics, the representation of black youth on the screen had come a long way since the days of Buckwheat.

Jaleel White (b. 1976) as Steve Urkel on an episode of *Family Matters*.

In time children also had more playthings relevant to their identities, from the Keisha doll and Sun-Man to the M.C. Hammer doll and *The Games of Africa*. If a child *had* to have a Barbie, a G.I. Joe® figure, or a Cabbage Patch Kid—and later, a Rugrat—many parents were glad they could get these dolls in caramel or chocolate.

Clockwise from above: Nakia (2000), a Get Real Girl action figure, inspired by basketball referee Karen Stroud, a former basketball player who grew up in Washington, D.C.; Tuskegee Bomber Pilot (1997), a member of the G.I. Joe crew; three-year-old Susie Carmichael, one of television's Rugrats™ with her own line of dolls and other toys; *The Games of Africa*, with playing pieces for Mancala, one of the oldest games in the world.

Decade after decade the number of books increased that black youth could feel good about reading, books that their white, Hispanic, Asian, and other-culture peers could learn from as well: from board books, picture books, and chapter books to poetry, novels, and nonfiction such as history and biography.

Over the years there also came several magazines targeted to the mind and imagination of young blacks. Examples include the exuberant *Ebony, Jr.!* (1973–1985). Another was *YSB* (*Young Sisters and Brothers*, 1991–1996). "Sportsbeat," "techno,"

Since the 1960s, books and magazines that speak to black children and mirror their lives have grown more common.

"work tip," "mo'money," "groomin'," and "bookin'" were among this national monthly's standard columns. As the magazine's editor, Frank Dexter Brown, pointed out in his first editorial, *YSB* was also "about history—indeed 'our' story. It's all in the mix. African roots, African American traditions."

As *YSB* trained and entertained, the magazine also created community, a vibe that prompted a fifteen-year-old girl from Alabama, to write to the editor: "I would like to see *YSB* start a pen pal section so your readers (including me) could have the opportunity to associate with other teens from around the country. . . . It would be great for building strong relationships with other sisters and brothers."

By the close of the twentieth century, black America had become more diverse, and naturally so had the lives of its ten million girls and boys. And the black child was perhaps the most multicultural child in America. He or she could have a family tree with long roots in America. Or be descended from blacks born in Africa or the Caribbean. Or be born of unions between an African American and an African or an

Afro-Caribbean, or between an African American, African, or Afro-Caribbean and someone of European or Asian descent. While some biracial children would opt to be "other," most regarded themselves as black.

There was diversity as well in standard of living. With the growth of the black middle class, there was a sizable number of children enjoying very comfortable, even pampered, lives. A great many others, however, were living desperate lives because they lived in poverty, with the cascade of problems that poverty brings.

Dancing at the Louvre by Faith Ringgold (1991). By the end of the twentieth century more and more black children were enjoying opportunities that their forbears never dreamed possible, from having pocket

When I was fourteen, I left an elitist public school with no racial sensitivity and went to an elitist private school with very few people of color. The logic behind this decision was that, while I wouldn't receive much racial support at the new school, at least I would receive a good education. Being one of the only black students was nothing new to me; being one of the only black students who wanted to be black did not come as a surprise either....

Racism was never overt at my school.... So when I asked the administration why Black History Month didn't exist at my school, they didn't consider it a deficiency on their part.

"There's really so much else going on right now," they said politely when I asked two years in a row. "But maybe we'll put an announcement in the bulletin."

And when I sat in the back of my freshman world history class, crying because the teacher had said slavery really wasn't that bad, no one thought it constituted a problem....

As I struggled to maintain a positive identity at school, I was simultaneously forging an idea about my role in the black community. Bourgeois black society wasn't for me, I knew that. Whist and debutante balls didn't fit on my packed agenda of writing, dancing, and thinking....

At the same time, I could never fit into the "other" black community—the "others" on the margins, looking in on society as a whole with hungry eyes. I wasn't streetwise....

I knew I wanted to serve a community that had no use for me as an individual. There is a psychic peculiarity of being an outsider to an outsiders' group, and I spent most of high school feeling very peculiar.

• Caille Millner (b. 1979), who grew up in San Jose, California, and began her career in journalism as a teenager

Out of the shadows of this despair stepped the embodiment of young inner-city restless energy: the phenomenon early on known as "Break-Boy," and later, "B-Boy." Born in the late 1960s/early 1970s, there was no epic movement for B-Boy to hook into. There seemed to be nothing but a pox upon his house—in the South Bronx, in South Central L.A., in 5th Ward Houston, B-Boy couldn't do like a string of his peers in the 'hood and in the 'burbs who charted a course for Establishment; B-Boy didn't believe there was a place for him in that world—didn't think he was wanted anywhere but in jail. So he set his sights on a nation of his own. And in a bathroom or his own room, on a corner, up on a roof, in a basement, garage, or schoolyard, B-Boy started making music.

Graffiti "tags" such as this, which began popping up in urban America in the early 1970s, was the work of many a B-Boy and B-Girl.

B-Boy whipped out songs about life in the street, songs about wanting to be outta the street, songs about crazy, messed up "AmeriKKKa." He dressed it up with baggy clothes (all the better for a scowling pose) and conjured up a rash of defiant names: Grandmaster Flash, Rock Steady Crew, Cold Crush Brothers, The Treacherous Three, Kool Herc.

It was 1979 and the Sugar Hill Gang was blowing up the charts with "Rapper's Delight." They had taken Chic's "Good Times," a song that had been out for a while, but was still rocking, and turned it into a rap song. It changed the face of music and it was the Sugar Hill Gang, along with Afrika Bambaataa and the Zulu Nation, who got me into rap. . . .

I was 11 when I first saw the Sugar Hill Gang perform. It was at the old Harlem Armory, not too far from the Apollo. They had been promoting this concert for more than a month in my neighborhood. There were flyers on every tree, light post, and brick wall in St. Albans and I wanted to be there. Because for the first time, there was a form of music that literally spoke to me. Sugar Hill had my voice. They rapped about things I could relate to or wanted to relate to. They rapped about women and money, and about money and women. They had checkbooks, credit cards, cars, and clothes.

But I couldn't have cared less about the cars, the clothes, and even the women. What they really had that I wanted most was the power to say whatever they wanted. . . . I got into rap for the power. I wanted to be heard.

• James Todd Smith, better known as LL Cool J (b. 1968)

Scratching, breaking, trading phrases, B-Boy sparked new-jack movies and magazines, made new words—phat, peeps, dilly. He imbued flat words with nerve, verve—represent, recognize, shine. East Coast. West Coast. He walked the world—changing music, airwaves, brain waves, fashion. And because of B-Boy, American—and world—youth culture was radically changed. At the end of the twentieth century, B-Boy's sound was outselling rock and country music.

With the mainstreaming of rap and hip-hop culture and the intense promotion (and thus, popularity) of the raunchiest rappers, there was a perception that most black youth—and only black youth—were out of control and way-

Boy with Skateboard (1999) by Gerald H. Purnell. This boy checking out the urban landscape is streetwise and positive—he knows he has a tomorrow.

February 16, 1991

Dear Janice,

Rondah's deciding to go back to school had me thinking that I shouldn't waste the opportunity I have now to go to school. I don't remember mentioning that I'm in a special program at school that skips me from 7th to 9th grade. I never mentioned that at school I'm thought of as smart. Teachers think so, students think, nerd. I don't think I'm really a nerd, I just understand the work more than most kids do and I remember things well. Anyway, that's why I'm skipping a grade. The great thing about it is I get out of this dumpy school one year earlier. I can't say I'm definitely going to Bronx Science but it is a dream of mine. The only thing that I think would stop me is if I don't pass the admissions test. That's my one worry. I'll just have to study hard.

• Latoya Hunter (b. 1978)

Star Material (1997) by Mark Downey. This photograph was used on the cover of an EthnoGraphics greeting card, with the following message (written by Downey) inside: "It started with a shining, glowing smile . . . and then you set the world on fire."

Fourteen-year-old Ayinde Jean-Baptiste, one of the most memorable speakers at the Million Man March in Washington, D.C. (1995), photographed by Lester Sloan.

ward. White-owned media paid a disproportionate amount of attention to the negative activities of young blacks, from gang-related drive-by shootings to the fatal shooting in the fall of 1997 of a young Michigan man by an eleven-year-old boy. Not until a spate of tragic school shootings by white boys in the 1990s—especially the 1999 massacre at Columbine High in Littleton, Colorado—did many people acknowledge that "at-risk" did not apply to black youth alone.

In reality, as was the case with so many of their nonblack peers—from strangers to classmates, teammates, neighborhood and playground buddies—countless black girls and boys were doing well, and good. They were not babies making babies. They were not caught up in drugs and alcohol. They were not thugs. They were eager young souls being well tooled for life by committed parents and competent, caring teachers and librarians.

Among these many shining stars were Venus and Serena Williams on the tennis courts; Damien Walters, youth director of the National Action Network; and Maisha Moses and her work with the Algebra Project, the organization her father, Robert Moses, founded. Bearing witness, as well, were all the gold, silver, and bronze medalists in the NAACP's national Olympics of the Mind program, ACT-SO (Afro-Academic, Cultural, Technological, and Scientific Olympics). And of course there were all the children who were nurtured and thrived in numerous organizations such as Girls, Inc.; the Boys Choir of Harlem; the East End Neighborhood House in Cleveland, Ohio; the Boston-born National Ten Point Leadership Foundation; The Rites of Passage Shule based in Gettysburg, Pennsylvania; and the Omega Boys Club/Street Soldiers in San Francisco.

Exploring new worlds, David Brower, grandson of the legendary environmentalist David C. Brower, visits an ancient Native American cliff dwelling in Pueblo Canyon, Arizona (c. May 1996), photographed by Raymond K. Gehman. This image brings to mind the slave fort on Senegal's Gorée Island: in particular, the Door of No Return, which opened onto the sea, and through which unknown numbers of African men, women, and children passed when being loaded on slave ships for the Middle Passage. The similarity yet striking contrast in time, place, and context speaks to how far Africans in America have come.

Nearly four hundred years have passed since the first black child, William, was born in America. Through bondage and freedom, persecution and progress, millions of black girls and boys have made their way. They have toiled, romped, created, faced the nightmares, and dared to dream. Millions upon millions have grown up to become men and woman who, in turn, have raised up another generation. So today black children continue to march on toward new victories: with more than a few on the threshold of making history themselves.

December 1999

My name is Sydney Simone George and I am almost five years old. I am African American, but I am also part Trinidadian and part Jamaican. I want to be an artist because I like painting. I like to paint me and my family and tell stories with the pictures. I also like to paint the ocean, trees and the sky. I love to write and draw on my computer. I make colorful designs and all kinds of shapes like squares and circles and rectangles and then I mix them up. I use my imagination and make many new shapes. I also love cool clothes and I put outfits together for me, my little sister, Courtney Nia, and my dolls. My mom says I might be a fashion designer since they use a lot of the things I like in their work. I think I would love that. Maybe I can have more than one job. My dad says I can be anything I want to in the whole wide world.

• Sydney Simone George (b. 1995) of Washington, D.C.

Opposite page: *Baptism* (1989) by John Biggers.

Notes

Part I: Out of Africa

Page 13

"20. and odd Negroes." John Rolfe to Sir Edwin Sandys, Virginia, January 1620, quoted in Ivor Noël Hume, *The Virginia Adventure: Roanoke to James Towne, An Archaeological and Historical Odyssey* (Charlottesville: University of Virginia Press, 1997), p. 359.

Page 15

On Robert Carter's plans to buy three girls. Philip D. Morgan, *Slave Counterpoint: Black Culture in the Eighteenth-Century Chesapeake and Lowcountry* (Chapel Hill: University of North Carolina Press, 1998), pp. 379–80.

"It would be like . . . status." Philip D. Morgan, "Re: Robert Carter and purchase of slaves for his grandsons," E-mail to the author, 13 December 2000.

On young servants of George Washington's stepchildren. Morgan, *Slave Counterpoint*, p. 212.

Page 16–17

On Elias Ball II's purchase of children. Edward Ball, *Slaves in the Family* (New York: Farrar, Straus & Giroux, 1998), pp. 193–94, p. 90 ff.

Page 18

"a woman . . . farm." Thomas Jefferson, quoted in Morgan, *Slave Counterpoint*, p. 94.

Page 19

"The first . . . nine years old." Venture Smith, *A Narrative of the Life and Adventures of Venture, A Native of Africa: But Resident above Sixty Years in the United States of America* (1798), in Dorothy Porter, ed., *Early Negro Writing, 1760–1837* (Baltimore: Black Classic Press, 1995), p. 546.

Page 20

"The first object . . . suffocated." Olaudah Equiano, *The Interesting Narrative of the Life of Olaudah Equiano, or Gustavas Vassa, the African* (1789), in Yuval Taylor, ed. *I Was Born a Slave: An Anthology of Classic Slave Narratives.* Vol.1 (Chicago: Lawrence Hill, 1999), pp. 57–59.

Page 21

"Their griefs are transient." Thomas Jefferson, *Notes on the State of Virginia.* 1785. Reprint. (New York: Penguin, 1999), p. 146.

Page 22

On escape of Lucy. *South Carolina Gazette*, April 17–April 24, 1749.

On cooper and son. Morgan, *Slave Counterpoint*, p. 545.

On Esther. Ibid., p. 543.

Page 23

"I was born in Princeton . . . nineteen." Henry Trumbull, ed., *Life and Adventures of Robert Voorhis, the Hermit of Massachusetts.* (Providence, R.I.: n.p., 1829), p. 10.

On last will and testament of Thomas Hadden. Abstracts of wills on file in the Surrogate's Office, City of New York. Vol. VI, in *Collections of the New-York Historical Society*, 1896, vol. 30., pp. 53–54.

Page 24

On last will and testament of Benjamin Steymets. Abstracts of wills on file in the Surrogate's Office, City of New York. Vol. VI, in *Collections of the New-York Historical Society*, 1896, vol. 30., p. 167.

Page 25

On Matthew Ashby. Bonnie Newman Stanley, "Matthew Ashby," http://accessva.com:8100/pages/bhistory/1998/ashbyhtm. Also, Unsigned, "Matthew Ashby," http://www.history.org/people/bios/ bioash.htm

On significance of 150 pounds. Edwin J. Perkins, *The Economy of Colonial America* (New York: Columbia University Press, 1980), p. 151.

Part II: Longing for the Jubilee

Page 31

"Us made play houses . . . up." Manda Boggan. Federal Writers' Project interview, in Ira Berlin et al., eds., *Remembering Slavery: African Americans Talk about Their Personal Experiences of Slavery and Emancipation* (New York: The New Press, 1998), p. 41. Lightly edited for readability for all ages.

Page 33

Candis Goodwin on "Injuns an' soldiers." Charles L. Perdue Jr., et al. eds., *Weevils in the Wheat: Interviews with Virginia Ex-Slaves* (Charlottesville: University of Virginia, 1992), p. 109.

On Hilary Herbert's relationship with enslaved boy. Wilma King, *Stolen Childhood: Slave Youth in Nineteenth-Century America* (Bloomington: Indiana University Press, 1997), p. 55.

"My mama died . . . spin." Mary Island. Federal Writers' Project interview, in Berlin, et al., eds., *Remembering Slavery*, p. 95.

Page 34

John Smith's remembrance of work. Federal Writers' Project interview, in James Mellon, ed. *Bullwhip Days: The Slaves Remember* (New York: Weidenfeld & Nicholson, 1988), pp. 39–40. Lightly edited for readability for all ages.

"We didn't have hardly . . . dress." Emma Knight. Federal Writers' Project interview, in Berlin, et al., eds., *Remembering Slavery*, p. 92.

"They died in droves." John W. Blassingame, *Slave Community: Plantation Life in the Antebellum South*. Revised ed. (New York: Oxford University Press, 1979), p. 181.

Page 35

"Aunt Viney took . . . night." Robert Shepherd. Federal Writers' Project interview, in Mellon, ed., *Bullwhip Days*, p. 38. Lightly edited for readability for all ages.

On Rebecca Grant's remembrance of whipping. Federal Writers' Project interview, in Mellon, ed., *Bullwhip Days*, p. 41.

On Josiah Henson's remembrance of father's beating. Josiah Henson, *The Life of Josiah Henson, Formerly a Slave, Now an Inhabitant of Canada* (1849), in Taylor, ed., *I Was Born a Slave*, p. 725.

On Allen Wilson's remembrance of mother's beating. Federal Writers' Project interview, in Perdue, ed., *Weevils in the Wheat*, p. 327. Lightly edited for readability for all ages.

Page 36

On Hannah Chapman's remembrance of her father. Federal Writers' Project interview, in Berlin, et al., eds., *Remembering Slavery*, p. 145. Lightly edited for readability for all ages.

"but that the . . . buzzard's eggs." Katie Sutton. Federal Writers' Project interview, in Mellon, ed., *Bullwhip Days*, p. 39.

"[Missus] kept me . . . ready." Ike Simpson. Federal Writers' Project interview, in Mellon, ed., *Bullwhip Days*, p. 42. Lightly edited for readability for all ages.

Page 37–39

On Frank Bell's remembrance of his grandfather. Federal Writers' Project interview, in Berlin, et al., eds., *Remembering Slavery*, p. 131.

On Jacob Stroyer's remembrance of the bully Gilbert. Jacob Stroyer. *My Life in the South*. 4th ed. (Salem, Mass.: Newcomb & Gauss, 1898): pp. 9–12.

On Charity's attempted murder of owners. *Louisville Courier*. Clipping reproduced in Velma Maia Thomas, *Lest We Forget: The Passage from Africa to Slavery and Emancipation*. (New York: Crown, 1997): p. 15.

Page 39–40

On Frederick Douglass's self-education. Frederick Douglass, *Narrative of the Life of Frederick Douglass, An American Slave* (1845), in Taylor, ed., *I Was Born a Slave*, pp. 553–57.

On John Sella Martin and literacy among slaves. Janet Duitsman Cornelius, *When I Can Read My Title Clear: Slavery, Literacy, and Religion in the Antebellum South* (Columbia: University of South Carolina Press, 1991), pp. 59–84.

Page 41

"Well, daughter . . . story." Papa Dallas, quoted by Tonea Stewart in Berlin et al., eds., *Remembering Slavery*, p. 280.

Page 43–47

Letters of Cincinnati children. Anonymous in Aptheker, ed., *A Documentary History*, p. 158.

On militancy of young Alexander Crummell and George T. Downing. Wilson Jeremiah Moses, *Alexander Crummell: A Study of Civilization and Discontent* (Amherst: University of Massachusetts Press, 1992), pp. 11–18.

On Rosetta Douglass's experience at Seward Seminary. Frederick Douglass. Letter to Horatio G. Warner, editor of *Rochester Courier*, Rochester, September 1848 (first published in *The Liberator*, October 6, 1848), in Herbert Aptheker, ed., *A Documentary History of the Negro in the United States*. Vol. 1 (Secaucus, N.J.: Citadel Press, 1951), pp. 274–77.

Page 49

"How bright . . . Dickens." Charlotte Forten. Reprinted in Brenda Stevenson, ed., *The Journals of Charlotte Forten Grimké* (New York: Oxford University Press, 1988), p. 59.

"I am very pleased . . . resolution." Letter from Euphemia Toussaint to her Uncle Pierre Toussaint, 25 December 1822, in Ellen Tarry, *Pierre Toussaint: Apostle of Old New York*. 2nd ed. (Boston: Pauline Books & Media, 1998), p. 260.

"During [my senior] year . . . told." Marticha Lyons, *Memories of Yesterdays: All of Which I Saw and Part of Which I Was* (n.p.,1928). Schomburg Center for Research in Black Culture.

Page 52
"One of the first . . . Yankees." Mary Barbour. Federal Writers' Project interview in Belinda Hurmence, ed., *My Folks Don't Want Me to Talk about Slavery* (Winston-Salem: John F. Blair, 1988), pp. 14–15.

Page 58
George Wells's letter. George Wells. Reprinted in Dorothy Sterling, ed., *The Trouble They Seen: The Story of Reconstruction in the Words of African Americans* (New York: Da Capo, 1994), p. 294.

Part III: Lift Every Voice and Sing

Page 64
Charles Johnson on "Lift Every Voice and Sing." Charles Johnson. "An Ever-Lifting Song of Black America," *New York Times*, 14 February 1999, pp. 1, 34.

Page 67
"I have never seen . . . things. M. H. Griffin, quoted in James D. Anderson, *The Education of Blacks in the South, 1860–1935* (Chapel Hill: University of North Carolina Press, 1988), p. 162.
"We lived just outside . . . warm." John Henrik Clarke, "A Search for Identity," in *New Dimensions in African History* (Trenton, N.J.: Africa World Press, 1991), p. 134.

Page 69
"Clumped in the vastness . . . money." Gordon Parks, *Voices in the Mirror* (New York: Doubleday, 1990), pp.1–2.
On Delany Sisters' memory of grocery shopping. Sarah L. Delany and A. Elizabeth Delany with Amy Hill Hearth. *Having Our Say: The Delany Sister's First 100 Years* (New York: Dell, 1994), p. 97

Page 70
"Success in life . . . impress." Paul Robeson, *Here I Stand*. 3rd ed. (Boston: Beacon Press, 3rd ed. 1988), p. 18.

Page 72
"I was interested in . . . us." Morgan Smith, quoted in *Harlem: The Vision of Morgan and Marvin Smith* (Lexington: University of Kentucky Press, 1998), pp.4–5.

Page 73
I remember . . . well." Margery Wheeler Brown. "Gifts from My Parents," in Wade Hudson and Cheryl Willis Hudson, eds. *In Praise of Our Fathers and Our Mothers: A Black Family Treasury by Outstanding Authors and Artists* (East Orange, NJ: Just Us Books, 1997), pp. 13–14.

Page 74
A doodlebug is together." Bessie Nickens, *Walking the Log: Memories of a Southern Childhood* (New York: Rizzoli, 1994), p. 19.

Page 75
"Well, Billikens . . . snow." Willard Motley, *The Defender Junior* (in *The Chicago Defender*), 6 January 1923.

Page 76
"That was the . . . taps." Fayard Nicholas, quoted in Constance Valis Hall, *Brotherhood of Rhythm: The Jazz Tap Dancing of the Nicholas Brothers* (New York: Oxford University Press, 2000), p. 51.
"Generally, he was . . . *Our Gang* series." Donald Bogle, *Toms, Coons, Mulattoes, Mammies and Bucks: An Interpretive History of Blacks in American Films,* rev. ed (New York: Continuum, 1996), p. 7.

Page 77
"We were among . . . whist." Dorothy West, "Fond Memories of a Black Childhood," in *The Richer, The Poorer: Stories, Sketches and Reminiscences* (New York: Doubleday, 1995): p. 173.

Page 79
"They'd start you watching . . . always!" Pernella Ross, quoted in Elizabeth Clark-Lewis, *Living In, Living Out: African American Domestics and the Great Migration* (New York: Kondasha, 1996), p. 42.

Page 82–82
On Johnnetta Betsch Cole's remembrances of racism. Johnnetta B. Cole, *Conversations: Straight Talk With America's Sister President* (New York: Doubleday, 1993), pp. 11–13.

"When I went to school . . . them." Margaret Walker, "Growing Out of the Shadow," in Maryemma Graham, ed., *How I Wrote Jubilee and Other Essays on Life and Literature* (New York: The Feminist Press, 1990), p. 3–4.

Page 85
"I remember . . . blackness." Leon Walter Tillage, *Leon's Story* (New York: Farrar, Straus & Giroux, 1997),p. 3.
On Nancy Douglas Bowlin's pride in heritage. Interview with the author, July 1999.

Page 87
On Jim McWilliam's strike. James McWilliams. Letter to William Loren Katz, 15 November 1993, in William Loren Katz, *Eyewitness: A Living Documentary of the African American Contribution to American History* (New York: Touchstone, 1995), p. 433.
"These apparent senseless . . . struggle." Charles Hamilton Houston, quoted in Genna Rae McNeil, "Charles Hamilton Houston," in *Black Heroes of the 20th Century* (Detroit: Visible Ink Press, 1998), p. 332.

Page 90
"At 2:30 P.M. . . . school." Randall Robinson, *Defending the Spirit: A Black Life in America* (New York: Dutton, 1998), pp. 28–30.

Page 91
"As the search . . . boy." Joyce Ladner, quoted in Steven Kasher, *The Civil Rights Movement: A Photographic History, 1954–68* (New York: Abbeville Press, 1996), p. 11.

Page 93
"In 1957, while most teenage girls . . . children." Melba Patillo Beals, *Warriors Don't Cry* (New York: Washington Square Press, 1995), p.1

Page 96
On a May day in Los Angeles . . . classroom. Anthony Ross, "Little Tigers Don't Roar," in Holliday, ed., *Children of the Dream*, pp. 231–32.

Page 97
On Tracy Price Thompson's first day of school. Tracy Price Thompson, "Bensonhurst: Black and Then Blue" in Laurel Holliday, ed., *Children of the Dream* (New York: Pocket Books), pp. 172–181.

Page 98
"All around us . . . gone." Ronald K. Fitten, "First Lesson in Rage: Fascination Turned to Hate in 1967 Detroit Riot," in Holliday, ed., *Children of the Dream*, pp. 163, 166–67.

Page 100
"Before rap music . . . all." E. Ethelbert Miller, *Fathering Words: The Making of an African American Writer* (New York: St. Martin's Press), pp. 29-30.

Page 101
On Charles Johnson's love for comic books and cartooning. Rudolph P. Byrd, ed., *I Call Myself an Artist: Writings By and About Charles Johnson* (Bloomington: Indiana University Press, 1999), p. 8.

Page 107
"About history . . . traditions." Frank Dexter Brown, "In the Mix," *YSB*, September 1991.
"I would like . . . sisters and brothers." Letters to the Editor ("word"), *YSB*, February 1992, page 8.

Page 109
"When I was fourteen . . . peculiar." Caille Millner, "Black Codes: Behavior in the Post-Civil Rights Era," in Holliday, ed., *Children of the Dream*, pp. 396–97.

Page 111
"It was 1979 . . . heard." LL Cool J, from *I Make My Own Rules*, in Herb Boyd, ed., *Autobiography of a People: Three Centuries of African American History Told By People Who Lived It*. (New York: Doubleday, 2000), p. 454.

Page 113
"Dear Janice . . . study hard." Latoya Hunter, *The Diary of Latoya Hunter: My First Year in Junior High School* (New York: Crown, 1991), pp. 75–76.

Page 116
"My name is . . . world." Sydney Simone Green George, letter to the author, December 1999.

Selected Bibliography

Anderson, James D. *The Education of Blacks in the South, 1860–1935.* Chapel Hill: University of North Carolina Press, 1988.

Bearden, Romare, and Harry Henderson. *A History of African-American Artists, from 1792 to the Present.* New York: Pantheon, 1993.

Berlin, Ira. *Many Thousands Gone: The First Two Centuries of Slavery in North America.* Cambridge: Bellknap Press/Harvard University Press, 1998.

Berlin, Ira et al., eds., *Remembering Slavery: African Americans Talk About Their Personal Experiences in Slavery and Freedom.* New York: The New Press, 1998.

Berlin, Ira, and Leslie Rowland. *Families and Freedom: A Documentary History of African-American Kinship in the Civil War Era.* New York: The New Press, 1997.

Blassingame, John W. *The Slave Community: Plantation Life in the Antebellum South.* Revised ed. New York: Oxford University Press, 1979.

Bolden, Tonya. *Strong Men Keep Coming: The Book of African American Men.* New York: Wiley, 1999.

——. *The Book of African American Women: 150 Crusaders, Creators, and Uplifters.* Boston: Adams Media, 1996.

Boyd, Herb, ed. *Autobiography of a People: Three Centuries of African American History Told By People Who Lived It.* New York: Doubleday, 2000.

Campbell, D.C. Jr., and Kym S. Rice. *Before Freedom Came: African American Life in the Antebellum South.* Charlottesville: University Press of Virginia, 1991.

Christian, Charles M. *Black Saga: The African American Experience.* Boston: Houghton Mifflin, 1995.

Clark-Lewis, Elizabeth. *Living In, Living Out: African American Domestics and the Great Migration.* New York: Kondasha, 1996.

Cornelius, Janet Duitsman. *When I Can Read My Title Clear: Slavery, Literacy, and Religion in the Antebellum South.* Columbia: University of South Carolina Press, 1991.

Crisis. Special Issue: Twenty-fifth Anniversary of Brown Decision. June/July 1979.

Dinwiddie-Boyd, Elza. *Proud Heritage: 11,001 Names for Your African-American Baby.* New York: Avon, 1994.

Foner, Eric, and Olivia Mahoney. *America's Reconstruction: People and Politics after the Civil War.* Baton Rouge: LouisianaUniversity Press, 1997.

Holliday, Laurel, ed. *Children of the Dream.* New York: Pocket Books, 1999.

Horton, James Oliver. *Free People of Color.* Washington, D.C.: Smithsonian Institution Press, 1993.

Katz, William Loren. *Eyewitness: A Living Documentary of the African American Contribution to American History.* New York: Touchstone, 1995.

King, Wilma. *Stolen Childhood: Slave Youth in Nineteenth-Century America.* Bloomington: Indiana University Press, 1997.

Marten, James. *The Children's Civil War.* Chapel Hill: University of North Carolina Press, 1998.

McElroy, Guy C. *Facing History: The Black Image in American Art, 1710–1940.* San Francisco: Bedford Arts, 1990.

Mellon, James, ed. *Bullwhip Days: The Slaves Remember.* New York: Weidenfeld & Nicholson, 1988.

Morgan, Philip D. *Slave Counterpoint: Black Culture in the Eighteenth-Century Chesapeake and Lowcountry.* Chapel Hill: University of North Carolina Press, 1998.

Perdue, Charles L., et al., eds. *Weevils in the Wheat: Interviews with Virginia Ex-Slaves.* Charlottesville: University of Virginia, 1992.

Pierson, William D. *From Africa to America: African American History from the Colonial Era to the Early Republic, 1526–1790.* New York: Twayne, 1996.

Reiss, Oscar. *Blacks in Colonial America.* Jefferson, N.C.: McFarland, 1997.

Sterling, Dorothy, ed. *The Trouble They Seen: The Story of Reconstruction in the Words of African Americans.* New York: Da Capo, 1994.

Taylor, Yuval, ed. *I Was Born a Slave: An Anthology of Classic Slave Narratives.* 2 vols. Chicago: Lawrence Hill Books,1999.

Werner, Emmy E. *Reluctant Witnesses: Children's Voices from the Civil War.* Boulder: Westview Press, 1998.

Wiggins, David K. "The Play of Slave Children in Plantation Communities of the Old South, 1820-60." *Growing up in America: Children in Historical Perspective.* eds. N. Ray Hiner and Joseph M. Hawes. Chicago: University of Illinois Press, 1985.

Wilson, Jackie Napoleon. *Hidden Witness: African-American Images from the Dawn of Photography to the Civil War.* New York: St. Martin's Press, 1999.

Wright, Donald R. *African Americans in the Colonial Era: From African Origins Through the American Revolution.* Wheeling, Ill.: Harlan Davidson, 1990.

Suggested Reading

Asante, Molefi Kete. *African American History: A Journey of Liberation* (2nd edition). Rochelle Park: People's Publishing, 2001.

Ayo, Yvonne. *Eyewitness: Africa*. London: Dorling Kindersley, 2000.

Barrett, Linda, and Casey King. *Oh, Freedom! Kids Talk About the Civil Rights Movement With the People Who Made It Happen*. New York: Knopf, 1997.

Benson, Kathleen, and James Haskins. *Bound for America: The Forced Migration of Africans to the New World*. New York: Lothrop, Lee & Shepard, 1999.

Benson, Kathleen, and James Haskins. *Building a New Land: African Americans in Colonial America*. New York: HarperCollins, 2001.

Carson, Clayborne, and Darlene Clark Hine, eds. *Milestones in Black American History*. Broomall: Chelsea House, 1994–1996.

Clinton, Catherine. *Scholastic Encyclopedia of the Civil War*. New York: Scholastic, 1999.

Feelings, Tom. *The Middle Passage: White Ships/Black Cargo*. New York: Viking, 1995.

Gorrell, Gena K. *North Star to Freedom: The Story of the Underground Railroad*. New York: Delacorte, 1997.

Hamilton, Virginia. *Many Thousand Gone: African Americans from Slavery to Freedom*. New York: Knopf, 1993.

Hansen, Joyce. *"Bury Me Not in a Land of Slaves": African-Americans in the Time of Reconstruction*. New York: Franklin Watts, 2000.

Hudson, Cheryl Willis, and Wade Hudson. *In Praise of Our Fathers and Our Mothers: A Black Family Treasury by Outstanding Authors and Artists*. East Orange: Just Us Books, 1997.

Johnson, Dinah. *All Around Town: The Photographs of Richard Samuel Roberts*. New York: Henry Holt, 1998.

Johnson-Feelings, Dianne. *The Best of the Brownies' Book*. New York: Oxford University Press, 1996.

Kelly, Robin D. G., and Earl Lewis, eds. *The Young Oxford History of African Americans*. New York: Oxford University Press, 1995–1997.

Lawrence, Jacob. *The Great Migration: An American Story*. New York: The Museum of Modern Art, The Phillips Collection, HarperCollins, 1993.

McKissack, Fredrick L. *Rebels Against Slavery: American Slave Revolts*. New York: Scholastic, 1996.

Myers, Walter Dean. *One More River to Cross: An African American Photography Album*. New York: HarperCollins, 1993.

Stanley, Jerry. *Hurry Freedom: African Americans in Gold Rush California*. New York: Crown, 2001.

Sullivan, Charles, ed. *Children of Promise: African-American Literature and Art for Young People*. New York: Harry N. Abrams, 1991.

Thomas, Velma Vaia. *Freedom's Children: The Passage from Emancipation to the Great Migration*. New York: Crown, 2000.

Thomas, Velma Maia. *Lest We Forget: The Passage from Africa to Slavery and Emancipation*. New York: Crown, 1997.

Watkins, Richard. *Slavery: Bondage Throughout History*. Boston: Houghton Mifflin, 2001.

Illustration Credits

The author is grateful to the following for use of their materials. (Items on pages 19, 26, 35, 39, 44 below, 84 above, and back flap are from the author's collection.)

Page numbers are used throughout the Illustration Credits for *Tell All the Children Our Story*

Bob Adelman: 95

American Antiquarian Society: 17, 21 left

Archive Photos: 65 (Frank Driggs), 97, 103 (Hulton), 104, 110 (Joan Slatkin)

The Art Museum, Princeton University. Gift of Mrs. Gerald Wilkinson: 14 left (Acc. #y1969-9), right (Acc. # y1969-10), photo by Clem Fiori

© Bettmann/Corbis: 89, 92

Index

Note: Page numbers in italics refer to illustrations

abolitionists, 26, 48
ACT-SO, 114
Adelman, Bob, 95
Africa: back-to-Africa movement,
    29; children kidnapped from,
    20, 21; slave houses in, *10;*
    slave trade in, 11–27
African Free Schools, 42, *42,* 44
African heritage, 85, 97, 99
Algebra Project, 114
Ali, Muhammad (Clay), *89*
Alston, Charles, 66
American Revolution, 26–27, 29
apprenticeship, 23, 55
Armstrong, Louis "Satchmo," 65, 80
Ashby, Mary and John, 24–25
Ashby, Matthew and Ann, 25

back-to-Africa movement, 29
Bailey, Fred, 39
Ball, Elias II, 16–17, *16*
Banjo Lesson, The (Tanner), *32*
Banneker, Benjamin, 25–26
Banneker, Molly and Bannka, 26
Banneker, Robert and Mary, 26
Baptism (Biggers), *117*
Barbour, Mary, 52
"Bars Fight" (ballad), 19, 21
Barton, Clara, 50
Beals, Melba Pattillo, 93
Beard, Matt Jr. "Stymie," 76
Bendolph, Artelia, *79*
Benezet, Anthony, *26,* 27
Bennett, Gwendolyn, 68
Biggers, John, 117
Birmingham, Alabama, 94–95, *95*
Birmingham News strike, 87
Black Church, roles of, 71, *72,* 73
Black Panthers, 96, 97
Black Power, 97, *97*
black pride, 97, 99
blacks: citizenship of, 30, 59; education
    of, 41–46; as entertainers, *32, 36,*
    76–77, *76, 77,* 110–12; free, 29,
    41–46, 55–56; inner-city energy of,
    110–12, 114; middle class, 44, 108;
    migrations of, 61, 80–81, *80, 81;*
    populations of, 29–30; in sports, 73,
    89, 102, *102;* voting rights for, 59
Blassingame, John W., 34
Boggan, Manda, 31
Bowlin, Nancy Douglas, 85, *85*
Boys Choir of Harlem, 114

Boy with Skateboard (Purnell), *112*
Boy with Tire (Lee-Smith), *88,* 89
Brandon, Brumsic Jr., 101
Braverman, Irwin, *2*
"Break-Boy" (B-Boy), 110–12
Bridges, Ruby, *94*
Brooks, James Henry "Jim Limber," *50*
Brooks, Rev. John, *71*
Brower, David, *115*
Brown, John, 48
Brown, John George, 61
Brown, Linda Carol, 88–89
Brown, Margery Wheeler, 73
Brown, Minnijean (Trickey), 93
Brown v. *Board of Education,* 89
Bunker family, boy as property of, *40*
Butcher, Solomon D., 59

Card Trick, The (Brown), *61*
Carnegie Foundation, 65
Carroll, Diahann, 104
Carter, Ralph, 104
Carter, Robert "King," 15, 18
Chapman, Hannah, 36
Charity (poisoner), 39
Child Life in Colonial Days (Earle), 18
children, *28;* bound out by parents, 25;
    chores of, 17–18, 19, 21, 25, 33, 34,
    47–48, *56, 78;* education of, *see*
    education; escorted to school, 46, *94;*
    kidnapped for slave trade, 20, 21;
    literature for, 84, *84,* 96, 106–7, *106;*
    multicultural, 107–8; of poverty, 47,
    78–80, *78, 79,* 108; purchase of,
    15–18, 21, 22; survival of, 34, 37, 50;
    television and, 103–4; toys and
    games of, 31, *31,* 33, 73–77, *74, 84,*
    99–100, *99, 105;* training of, 15;
    violence in lives of, 34–36, 56, 59
"Children's Crusade" (1963), 95
Christmas Morning Breakfast (Pippin),
    75
Civil Rights Acts, 59
civil rights crusade, 87–99
Civil War, 48, 50, 51, 54, *57*
Clarke, John Henrik, 67
Clay, Cassius (Muhammad Ali), *89*
coffle-yoke, *19*
Cole, Johnnetta Betsch, 82–83
Collins, Addie Mae, 94
Colored Waif's Home, 65
Columbian Orator, The, 39, *40*
Colvin, Claudette, 92
comic strips for, 100, *101*
Copage, Marc, 104
Coplan Family (Prior), *45*
Cornelius, Don, 103

Cosby, Bill, 104
cotton, 30, 33, 37, 80
Crandall, Prudence, *44*
Crummell, Alexander, 44, 46
Crummell, Boston, 44
Custer, George Armstrong, *50*

Dancing at the Louvre (Ringgold), *108*
Decker, Joseph, 8
Defender Junior, 75
Delany, Sadie and Bessie, 69
Doodlebug (Nickens), *74*
Double Dutch Series (Dunkley), *99*
Douglass, Frederick, 40, 48
Downey, Mark, 113
Downing, George T., 46–47
Draft Riots, New York, 49, 51
Dunkley, Tina, 99

Earle, Alice Morse, 18
East End Neighborhood House, 114
Eckford, Elizabeth, 93
Edgar, Medgar, 91
education: of free blacks, 41–46, 55–56;
    of individual children, 25–26, 39–40,
    47, 58; integration of, 89–90, 92–95,
    92, 94, 97; laws against, 40; punish-
    ment for, 40, 41; reaching one's
    potential via, 69–70, 113; sacrifices
    for, 67, 68; schools destroyed, 59;
    separate but equal, 64–70, *68, 70,*
    87–89, 97
Eisenhower, Dwight D., 93
Eldridge, Elleanor, 47–48
Elias Ball II (Theus), *16*
Emancipation Proclamation, 48
Equiano, Olaudah, 20, 21
Esther (runaway), 22

Farm Boy (Alston), *66*
Faubus, Orval, 93
Fauset, Jessie, 84
Feelings, Tom, 10
Fifteenth Amendment (1870), 59
Fitten, Ronald K., 98
Forbes, Edwin, 54
Ford, Ellis, 85
Forten, Charlotte, 45
Forten, James, 26–27, 45
Fort Mose, Florida, 22
Fourteenth Amendment (1868), 30, 59
free blacks, 29, 48; after Civil War,
    54–61; education of, 41–46
Freedom's Journal, 44

Gamin (Savage), *85*
Garnet, Henry Highland, 44

Garrison, William Lloyd, 48
Gehman, Raymond K., 115
George, Sydney Simone, 116
Girl at Gee's Bend, Alabama
  (Rothstein), *79*
Girls, Inc., 114
Gomez, Wendel, 2
Goodwin, Candis, 33
graffiti "tags," *110*
Grant, Rebecca, 35
Grant, Gen. Ulysses S., 54
Great Migration, 61, 80–81, *80, 81*
Green, Ernest, 93

Hadden, Thomas, 23
Hall, Primus, 42
Hayes, Rutherford B., 61
Henry, Edward Lamson, 60
Henry Darnall III as a Child (Kühn), *16*
Henson, Josiah, 35
Herbert, Hilary, 33
Hine, Lewis, 68
Hoskins, Allen Clayton "Farina," 76
Houston, Charles Hamilton, 87
Hughes, Langston, 2, 84, *86*
Hunter, Latoya, 113

indentured servants, 13–14
Island, Mary, 33

Jackson 5, *103*
James, bill of sale for, *25*
Jamestown Landing (Pyle), *12, 13*
Jean-Baptiste, Ayinde, *114*
Jeanes Fund, 65
Jefferson, Thomas, 26
Johnson, Charles, 64, *101*
Johnson, Eastman, 53
Johnson, James Weldon, 63–64
Jones, Absalom, 42
Jones, Lois Mailou, 84

Kaplow, Isidor, *2*
Kept In (Henry), *60*
King, Martin Luther Jr., 94, 95
King, Susie, 50
Kitt, Eartha, 80
Knight, Emma, 34
Kühn, Justus Engelhardt, 16
Ku Klux Klan, 80, 82, 83, 95

Ladner, Joyce, 91
LaGuardia, Fiorello, 76
Lee, Gen. Robert E., 54
Lee, Russell, 86
Lee-Smith, Hughie, 89
"Lift Ev'ry Voice and Sing" (Johnson),
  63–64
Lincoln, Abraham, 48, 63
"Little Rock Nine," 93
LL Cool J (Smith), 111
Louis, Joe "Brown Bomber," 73

"Luther" (Brandon), *101*
Lyons, Maritcha, 49, *49*

McGee, Paula and Pamela, *102*
McNair, Denise, 94
McVey children, *62*
McWilliams, Jim, 87
March on Washington for Jobs and
  Freedom, 94
maroon settlements, 22
Marshall, Thurgood, 89
Martha's Vineyard vacations, 77
Martin, John Sella, 40
Martin, Rowland J. Jr., *100*
"men-boys" (teenagers), 22
Middle Passage, 11–27
Middle Passage: White Ships/Black Cargo
  (Feelings), *10*
Miller, E. Ethelbert, 100
Miller, Lewis, 37
Million Man March, 114
Millner, Caille, 109
Moorhead, Scipio, *21*
Moses, Maisha, 114
Mothershed, Thelma (Wair), 93
Motley, Willard, 75
Mount Vernon, *24*

NAACP (National Association for the
  Advancement of Colored People),
  87, 89, 91, 114
National Action Network, 114
National Ten Point Leadership
  Foundation, 114
Negro Boys on Easter Morning (Lee), *86*
Negro History Week, 84, *86*
Negro League, 73
Negro Rural School Fund (Jeanes
  Fund), 65
Nell, William Cooper, 44
Nelson, Haywood Jr., 104
Newsome, Effie Lee, 84
Newton, Huey, 96
New York Manumission Society, 42
Nicholas, Fayard and Harold, 76, 77
Nickens, Bessie, 74
North America, slavery in, 14
Nursemaid and Her Charge, 34

Olympics of the Mind, 114
Omega Boys Club/Street Soldiers, 114
Our Gang (Decker), *8*
Our Gang movies, 76

Papa Dallas, 41
Parks, Gordon, 69, 80
Parks, Rosa, 92
Phelps-Stoke Fund, 65
Phillips, Wendell, 48
Pippin, Horace, 75
plantations: slave labor used on, 15, *56*;
  slave quarters of, *18, 31, 38*

Plessy v. *Ferguson*, 64, 89
Porter, James A., 82
Portrait of a Negro Boy (Zechel), *14*
Portrait of a Negro Girl (Zechel), *14*
poverty, children of, 47, 78–80, *78, 79,*
  108
Powell, Rev. Adam Clayton Sr., 72
Prince, Lucy Terry, 19
Pringle, Robert, 22
Prior, William Matthew, 45
Problem We All Live With, The
  (Rockwell), *94*
Purnell, Gerald H., 112
Pyle, Howard, 13

race hatred, violence of, 82–83, 92–95
racial discrimination, 61, 83; in
  beauty standards, 84–85; in
  literature, 84, 96
"Rapper's Delight" (Sugar Hill
  Gang), 111
Ray, Gloria (Karlmark), 93
Reason, Patrick Henry, 42
Reconstruction (1863-1877), 55–56
Ride for Liberty, A (Johnson), *53*
Ringgold, Faith, 108
Rites of Passage Shule, 114
Roberts, Terrence, 93
Robertson, Carole, 94
Robeson, Paul, 39, 70
Robeson, William Drew, 39, 70
Robinson, Randall, 90
Rockwell, Norman, 94
Rosenwald, Julius, Fund, 65, 67
Ross, Anthony, 96
Ross, Pernella, 79
Rothstein, Arthur, 79

sampler, *42*
Sanderson, Jeremiah Burke, 42
Savage, Augusta, 85
Savage, Edward, 24
Schuyler, Philippa Duke, 76, 77
Shackelford, Jane D., 84
Shepherd, Robert, 35
Sheppard, W. L., 57
Simpson, Ike, 36
slavery: abolition of, 30, 54, 59;
  beginnings of, 13–14; opponents of,
  26, 48; and race prejudice, 83
slaves: advertised in newspapers, *15,
  17, 37*; birth of, 15; bought out of
  bondage, 44; children as, *see*
  children; in Civil War, 50; escaping,
  22, 39, *53*; freed on owner's death,
  23, 24; living quarters of, *18, 31, 38,
  54*; populations of, 29–30; purchase
  of, 15–18, 24; smuggled into U.S.,
  46; taken out of Africa, 11–27;
  uniting with family, 54–55; whips,
  35; yokes, *19*

Slave's Friend, The, 44
slave ships, 11, *12*, 13, 16, 18, 20, *27*
slave trade, 11–27
Slave Trader (Miller), *37*
Sloan, Lester, 114
Smith, James Todd (LL Cool J), 111
Smith, John, 34
Smith, Marvin and Morgan, 72
Smith, Venture (Broteer), 18, 19
Speese, Moses, and family, *59*
Spencer, Danielle, 104
Spurr, Samuel, 25
Star Material (Downey), *113*
Stewart, Tonea, 41
Steymets, Benjamin, 24
Stroud, Karen, 105
Stroyer, Jacob, 39
Sugar Hill Gang, 111
Supreme Court, U.S., 64, 89, 90, 93
Sutton, Katie, 36

Tanner, Henry Ossawa, 32
Tappen, Lucia, 49
television, 103–4
Theus, Jeremiah, 16
Thirteenth Amendment (1865), 59
Thomas, Billie "Buckwheat," 76
Thomas, Ernest, 104
Thomas, Jefferson, 93

Thompson, Tracey Price, 97
Till, Emmett, murder of, 91
Tillage, Leon Walter, 85
Toussaint, Euphemia, *47*
TransAfrica, 90
Trusty, Rachel, 48
Tucker, William (first African
    American), 13, 116
Turner, Nat, 48
Two Boys in the Slave Fort (Feelings), *10*
Tyson, Neil de Grasse, 102

Underground Railroad, *39*, 44, 49
urban riots, 49, 51, 97–98

vaudeville, 76, *76*, 77
View of Mount Vernon from the Northeast
    (Savage), *24*
Viney, Aunt, 35
violence: after Civil War, 56, 59;
    Emmett Till murder, 91; of race
    hatred, 82–83, 92–98; to slaves,
    34–36; of urban riots, 49, 51, 97–98
Voorhis, Robert, 23
voting rights, 59

Walker, Jimmy, 104
Walker, Margaret, 83
Walls, Carlotta (LaNeir), 93

Walters, Damien, 114
Washington, George, 15, 24
Washington, James B., *50*
Waud, Alfred R., 55
Weems, Anna Maria, *39*
Wells, Ebenezer, 19
Wells, George, 58
Welsh, Molly, 26
Wesley, Cynthia, 95
West, Dorothy, 77
Wheatley, John, *21*
Wheatley, Phillis, *21*
When the Klan Passes By (Porter), *82*
whip, *35*
White, Jaleel, *104*
Whiting, Adele, 84
Wiggins, Thomas Greene Bethune, *36*
Williams, Venus and Serena, 114
Wilson, Allen, 35–36
"women-girls" (teenagers), 22
Woodson, Carter G., 84
World War II, 87
Wright, Richard, 80

YMCA city cleanup, *71*
yoke, *19*
YSB, 106–7

Zechel, Charles (Carolus), 14